THE · ART · OF
SELLING

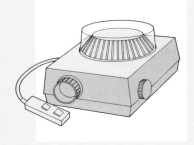

Create the Idea

THE · ART · OF
SELLING

MALCOLM BIRD

HEADLINE

A QUARTO BOOK

Copyright © 1991 Quarto Publishing plc
First published in Great Britain in 1991
by HEADLINE BOOK PUBLISHING PLC

British Library Cataloguing in Publication Data
Bird, Malcolm
The Art of Selling
1. Salesmanship
I. Title
658. 8′5

ISBN 0–7472–0203–6

This book was designed and produced by
Quarto Publishing plc
The Old Brewery
6 Blundell Street
London N7 9BH

Senior editor Sally MacEachern
Project editor Emma Callery
Designer Graham Davis
Photographers Ian Howes, Martin Norris, Paul Forrester
Illustrators Stuart Robertson, Rob Shone, Dave Kemp
Picture manager Joanna Wiese
Picture research Arlene Bridgewater, Emma Callery
Art director Moira Clinch
Publishing director Janet Slingsby

Manufactured in Hong Kong by Regent Publishing Services Ltd
Typeset by Ampersand Typesetting Ltd, Bournemouth
Printed in Hong Kong

HEADLINE BOOK PUBLISHING PLC
Headline House
79 Great Titchfield Street
London W1P 7FN

THE THREE KEYS

Presentations which bring results are always based on three key requirements: preparation, transmission and assimilation. Knowing how to use the three keys is the first and most essential step towards getting real results.

Business and sales presentations can be made in a wide variety of ways and in a variety of situations. The active presenter may, on one day, be talking (and hopefully listening) to a prospective customer across the latter's desk. On the next day the presentation may be in an hotel conference suite to, say, a dozen buyers from a dozen different companies – or the salesperson may be addressing an audience of several hundred in a large auditorium. These examples are just highlights from a whole range of possibilities, which can vary from training in-house staff to reporting back to shareholders at the AGM.

The truly professional presenter will take all these opportunities in his or her stride and be aware of the techniques needed to succeed with each one.

Fortunately for anyone who needs to sell to survive, the basic principles of effective presentation are the same whatever the circumstances. Naturally enough, differing situations demand substantial differences in style of presentation – and cost – but the target is the same in each case. Sales are achieved by making an *effective communication* which is planned and carried out from the *customer's viewpoint*.

A presentation made in a muddled, unplanned fashion from the viewpoint of the seller is unlikely to succeed – unless the audience happens to be unusually bright, patient and forgiving. Those characteristics cannot be relied on, since few buyers have the time or inclination to listen to a poor presentation and work out for themselves the reasons why they should buy the product or service. It is much more likely that they will "switch off" after two or three minutes and take their business to another company.

NOTE: *The cumbersome terms his/hers, he/she etc., have been avoided in this book. Unless the context indicates the contrary, all masculine gender words should be taken as meaning both genders.*

THE THREE KEYS

Educational psychologists tell us that someone listening to an explanation of a subject for the first time is likely to assimilate only about 30% of what he or she was told. In other words, about 70% will be either misunderstood, incomprehensible or forgotten. The experts also tell us that the percentages can be reversed if the right techniques are used, so that 70% is assimilated and only 30% is lost.

No one can prove that these figures are exact or what the figures really will be in any particular case. However, since we have all experienced the agony of poor presentations, as well as the ease with which we understand a well-expressed message, common sense

The right techniques can increase your score rate. Your audience can be made more receptive of your message and will remember more of it.

tells us that the psychologists are essentially correct.

In every case, we need our listeners to comprehend and remember as much as possible of our message and certainly enough to bring them to a "buy decision".

Achieving this depends on three key elements – Preparation, Transmission and Assimilation. All these elements are clearly linked, with the second heavily dependent on the first and Assimilation dependent on Preparation and Transmission.

PREPARATION

The success rate in putting over a message is directly proportional to the time and effort put into preparing for it. The opposite is also true, as was demonstrated by the salesman who gave a 30-minute talk on the chemicals he was trying to sell to a group of people from a potentially large customer. The salesman talked with great confidence about the price advantages he could offer and the first-rate packaging and delivery services on which his company prided itself.

The audience listened politely and then began to ask technical questions about the characteristics of the products. The salesman was not especially well informed on some of these topics. He muddled through for a time and then offered to send leaflets describing the specifications and other scientific details.

The presentation was a disaster. *All* the people in the audience were technical specialists (chemists and chemical engineers) whose main or sole interest was in the technical matters. They were not interested in discount terms, distribution systems or packaging specifications. These topics were matters for the purchasing and

Preparation really counts. The amount of effort you invest in a presentation will be reflected in the quality of your performance.

accounts departments.

The salesman, whose personal credibility ended up at about 1 on a scale of 0–10, could have prevented the disaster by a few simple precautions:

A Finding out who he would be talking to and what their jobs were.

B Deciding what the listeners were likely to be most interested in.

C Arming himself with the relevant technical information and making it the main theme of his talk.

If he had been unable to find out in advance what sort of people would be listening to him, he could have prepared for all eventualities and made himself familiar with all the features of his company and products. This might have meant a lot of extra work for the salesman, but it could also have provided a lot of extra sales. There is, in any case, no excuse for lack of product knowledge.

What then should be considered in the preparation stage? The following are the main items for preliminary consideration:

● Will the listeners be familiar with the trade or technical jargon you normally use, or should you allow for an audience which is new to the subject?

● How much time will be needed? Bearing in mind that 40 minutes is about all that most people will tolerate in one session, should the presentation be broken up with a coffee break, lunch or a second speaker?

● What are the aspects which the listeners will be most interested in? Accountants will be looking at the cost aspects, lawyers will be interested in the legal, production people thinking about machine downtime, reject rates and delivery schedules.

● What proof will be needed that the product or service actually works? A demonstration or factual experiences of previous customers may be needed.

● How can the presentation be made exciting and lively (if that is suitable for the audience concerned)?

● Where, if there is a choice, should the presentation take place? The convenience of the customers is vital. Ideally, they should be in surroundings in which they are relaxed, and not restricted.

● When should the presentation be made? Again, consider what is most convenient for the customers. Should the "graveyard" period immediately after lunch be avoided?

● What questions are likely to be asked? Not having the answer to a reasonable question is not just embarrassing – it can deal a death blow to a sale or to several sales.

● Should the presentation be regarded as a stage in a series of steps which will lead to a sale? Not all sales are made at the first attempt, and there are occasions when it is positively counter-productive to try to do so.

● How will the presentation look from the customer's angle? This is the most important item of preparation of all. There is no reason

Adequate preparation may mean that a mass of disparate information has been condensed into one easily presented and assimilated visual.

on earth why customers should see things from the salesperson's point of view. If they see, or even suspect, that it is only your needs and ideas which are being taken into account, you can say "goodbye" to their willing attention. How would you feel if someone tried to sell you something simply on the basis of what he or she thought was a good idea?

● Is the presentation intended to inform, persuade or sell? The approach will depend on the results required.

TRANSMISSION

Having worked methodically through the preparation stage, many of the potential pitfalls will have been spotted and can be avoided. In addition, some of the requirements in the transmission stage will have emerged. For example, the realization that what you want to say involves some complicated financial figures suggests finding an easily understood way to say it. A carefully prepared visual aid, such as a table of costs clearly visible on a screen, will be much easier to take in than a verbal string of figures fired rapidly at the audience.

This is particularly true if you are addressing people in a language not their own, when numbers are particularly difficult to comprehend.

What then are the basic rules of transmission of the message?

● Keep it simple. Avoid long words or fancy terminology. Some sales people are tempted to go over the top with what they think are impressive sounding expressions. This form of showing off should be avoided, if only because it makes it harder for audiences to understand what is being said. In addition to the fact that listeners may *misunderstand,* anything that makes them work harder will probably annoy them.

Another possible penalty for a complicated explanation is that listeners who do not understand it may feel embarrassed or even guilty. They might feel that they *should* understand and will not be pleased with a salesperson who makes them aware of their shortcomings – real or imagined.

● Keep it short. Any unnecessary material in your presentation means unnecessary work for the listeners. Work makes people tired, and tired people stop listening.

● Be enthusiastic. Dull, unexcited talkers end up with bored, unexcited listeners.

● Vary the pitch of your voice when addressing an audience. Lengthy monotones send people to sleep.

● Take your time. Talking too fast can put a strain on your audience.

● Avoid dashing from one topic to another. Make sure that the listeners are ready to move to the next point.

● Use humour with care. Some speakers can keep an audience spellbound with their wit – but not many. If you are not one of those people who can automatically and instinctively come up with throwaway lines or amusing asides, don't try it. Contrived humour sounds contrived, reduces the speaker's credibility and loses the attention of the audience.

● *Never ever* make jokes about sex, religion, race, politics or any other sensitive subject. A

Be careful not to build a wall between yourself and the audience with confusing facts or too much data. Visual aids help to break down barriers.

Presentations should be lively and entertaining. A few surprises or an eye-catching illustration can work wonders with an audience.

young salesman making his very first call told a "funny" story with a religious content. He lost the account and later found out that the potential customer was a lay preacher who regarded the joke as blasphemous! You can of course make a joke or two about yourself – if desirable and if it is really funny.

● Don't distract the audience.

An otherwise first class speaker had, until he saw himself on a video, a habit of mopping his brow with a handkerchief. The handkerchief, used frequently, was returned to a different pocket after each use. The audience would invariably find this fascinating. They would follow the handkerchief from pocket to pocket, trying to guess which one it would go into next. It was no doubt entertaining, but it also distracted the audience from what the speaker was saying.

Another, experienced, speaker was prone to repeating the words "Ladies and Gentlemen" in the course of his talks. The audience were treated to something like this:

"Ladies and gentlemen, the product we wish to talk about is, ladies and gentlemen, the latest development which as you know, ladies and gentlemen, has come from our research laboratories, ladies and gentlemen..."

Some of the audience would invariably find the repetition irritating. Some would begin to count the repetitions. Just about all were distracted from the message.

Other self-made distractions include:

Jangling keys or coins in a pocket.

Repeatedly clearing your throat.

Pacing up and down like a caged tiger.

Posturing: the Napoleonic hand in the jacket or the prosecuting lawyer's grip on the lapels are well used poses.

Waving your arms about.

Picking fluff from a sleeve.

And, sin of sins, picking your nose or scratching your backside. All of these distractions are taken from real life, as anyone who has sat in a classroom will know.

● Be absolutely honest. Never exaggerate or make claims you cannot support. You will be found out in the end, and the damage can be substantial.

Avoid overuse of words like "very", "amazing", "tremendously" and "incredibly".

It is more effective to say "This machine works at high speed even in cold conditions" than to invite cynical responses by saying "This machine works at a tremendously high speed even in incredibly cold conditions".

The listener's idea of what is amazing,

Jokes can be an asset – if you are expert at using them. The wrong joke can be disastrous. Avoid sex, race and politics and stick to safe areas.

tremendous and incredible may be quite different from yours. Don't tempt him to say so.

● Don't use canned sales talks. A spiel learned by heart sounds exactly what it is – unless it is used by a skilled actor.

The professional salesperson will know the product and make preparations so thoroughly that he will be able to say whatever is necessary off-the-cuff. This is more impressive and sounds more convincing.

If you *must* have a canned presentation, you might as well have it printed in a glossy brochure and mail it to the customer. The effect is much the same and the cost could be less.

● Don't read from a script. Reading from a script is a canned sales talk which has not been memorized. A few notes on a card *are* a good idea to help you keep the presentation moving in a logical sequence (another essential requirement) and to avoid leaving something out. This is all you need.

● Avoid clichés. "Unaccustomed as I am to public speaking" is a terrible way to start any presentation. So is, "Can you hear me at the back?"

Another piece of preparation

There is no substitute for practice in putting over your piece. The quality of transmission can be improved by practice, and a few sessions with a video camera can work wonders. Role playing with colleagues can be hard going – and reveal all your weak points – but it is better to do it in your own office or training room than in front of customers.

Sorting out the weaknesses and polishing the performance before meeting the customers will also improve the salesperson's confidence. A high degree of self confidence is apparent to the customers and it encourages their confidence in you and therefore in your product. Your nervousness can make the customer wary and nervous, too.

ASSIMILATION

If your preparation was good and your transmission effective, it is likely that the customer's assimilation level will be high. However, there are still a number of things which can be done to ensure a really good job.

Once again, think from the listeners' viewpoint. Consider the things which may inhibit their assimilation. They include:

● BOREDOM A dull or long presentation will promote boredom as much as one which is too highbrow or too lowbrow.

Any material which is irrelevant – or which the customer *thinks* is irrelevant – will also cause eyelids to drop and brains to slip into neutral.

● FATIGUE Listeners can become exhausted if the session goes on too long – if boredom doesn't get them first. They can also be worn out by complicated material – especially if it is presented too quickly.

● FEAR It may sound strange to list fear on the part of the customers as a problem. After all, you are not likely to ask for an order with a shotgun aimed at the customers (are you?).

There are nevertheless some psychological shotguns which can cause fear. One is the fear that you will ask people to comment publicly on their reaction to the product.

Try to anticipate any obstacles to your listeners' ability to assimilate your message.

Good visuals will assist assimilation and help to prevent the onset of boredom. A visualizer (right) is a very effective means of projecting an image with a minimum amount of effort, and is ideal for use with a small group.

Undue pressure can also cause fear —
including pressing customers to try out your
product in front of everyone else. They
may be terrified of making a mistake and
losing face.

● DISTRACTION (again). A major sales
presentation was given to a largely male
audience in a well equipped conference hall.
All went well until the audience was invited to
put questions to the panel of speakers. Then
the presenters noticed that the bulk of the
audience was watching in fascination the
pretty and scantily dressed girls who took
microphones from place to place in the
audience. Not only were many of the answers
to the questions ignored, but some of the
questions clearly showed that the girls had
been distracting the audience while they had
been standing by during the presentation.

Less dramatic distractions can include:

● Uncomfortable seating.
● Poor ventilation.
● Temperature too high or too low.
● Lack of comfort breaks.
● Noises off and whistling microphones.

These are all causes of distraction *in addition*
to those which the salesperson may introduce
personally. Ideally, they will all be prevented
by attention to detail at the preparation stage.

● TRANSMISSION STYLE. All the negative factors
already mentioned under transmission will
inhibit assimilation. The most important are
muddled presentations with subjects in
an illogical sequence, and a dull and
uninspired speaker.

Avoiding these obstacles to assimilation is
vital if you are to succeed.

**It is important to give your
presentation in a venue where
there will be minimal
distraction. Bad lighting,**
**uncomfortable seating, poor
ventilation or extremes in
temperature will affect the
audience's concentration.**

PLANNING YOUR OPTIONS

This chart is designed to provide an at-a-glance overview of the suitability of a particular piece of equipment for your presentation. The symbols are representative rather than exact, enabling you to make a quick assessment of factors such as cost or ease of use.

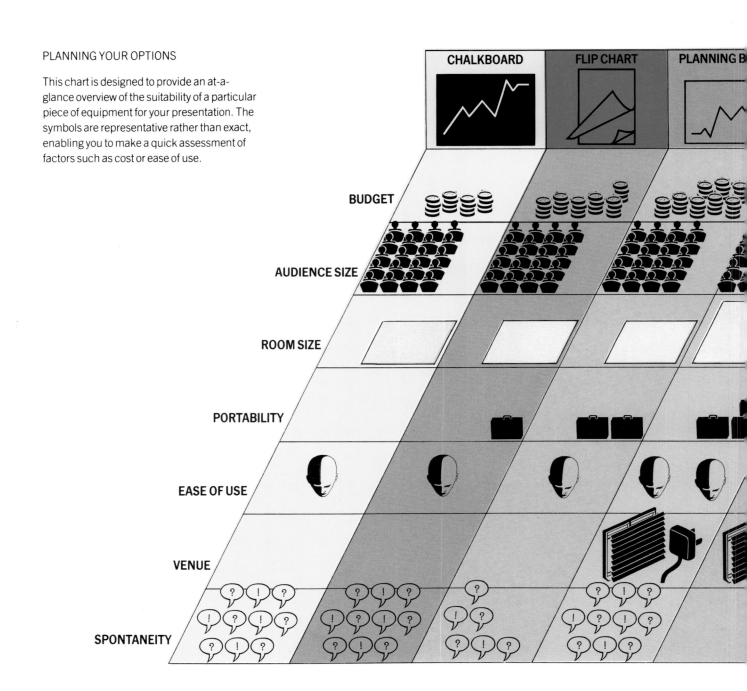

OHP	SLIDES	OHP + COMPUTER	VIDEO	REMOTE DISPLAY	MULTI-MEDIA

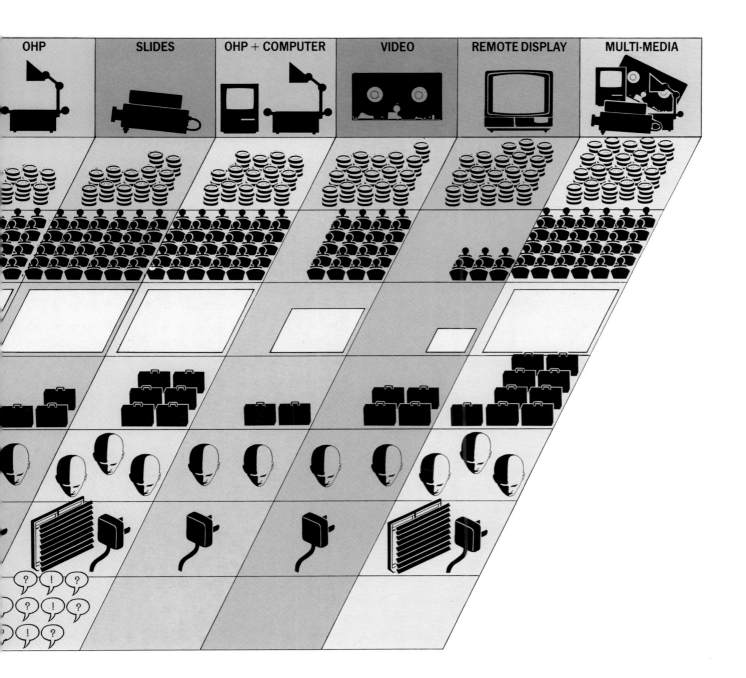

<u>THE</u>
PSYCHOLOGY

Presenters ignore the psychological aspects at their peril. Whether you are facing one person, a small group or a large gathering, always remember that you are talking to individuals and tailor your approach accordingly.

Presentations happen in two distinct forms – one-on-one (person to person) and multiples (one or more people presenting to a group). Although this book concentrates on multiple presentation, it is vital to understand that you are always "selling to individuals". Groups are made up of individuals and, to a large extent, should be treated as such. It is important to be well aware of the factors that will influence the *individuals* in your audience and to allow for them in everything you do or say.

The most important underlying influence on the individuals in your audience will be emotion.

People rarely buy as a result of an exercise of pure logic and it is probable that some people scarcely use logic at all. Emotion is one of the most powerful influences on buyers (and sellers) and recognizing both the problems and the opportunities this brings is a "must" for the salesperson.

The powerful effect of emotion on a buying decision is often hidden. Take for example the case of someone buying a car. On the face of it the would-be purchaser is acquiring a means of transport and should be taking into account such features as reliability, power ratio, braking efficiency, fuel consumption, ease of repair and so on. These may indeed be considerations in the buyer's mind but at least equally important are:

● STYLE Will the buyer look impressive behind the wheel? Will the shape and general design say "This car is owned by a successful person with flair and charisma" or will it say "This dull looking vehicle is the type owned by dull and unadventurous people"?

● STATUS Will the car "keep up with the Jones's"? Is it big enough to look impressive?

Does it have some fancy extras to make it more noticeable or more expensive looking?

● LIFESTYLE Does the car fit in with the way you want to live? Does it represent a young, adventurous and lively lifestyle or is it more suggestive of the married couple with two kids and a mortgage?

All these thoughts go through the mind of the car buyer and have nothing whatsoever to do with the technical qualities of the car. Thus, like many products and services it is a means to an end not an end in itself. The sale may depend on satisfying this emotional need and it is the "end" that needs to be presented and demonstrated not just the means to it.

This principle applies when selling industrial products and services to industrial buyers – as do many others resulting from the emotional side of the human animal. They will come up again and again in the various sales situations in which the seller can find himself.

APPEARANCE

Immediately you walk into the presence of potential customers – even before you have

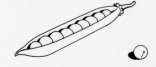

What will your audience expect you to look like? Meeting expectations will encourage them to trust you.

said a word – you could be making a sale easier or more difficult simply because of the way you appear to them.

People feel more comfortable and trusting with those who are either like themselves, or what they think the other person should look like.

It is no accident that in Hollywood films made for American consumption the "goodies" are clearly American. The "baddies"? They have foreign accents. In every "historical" film this is very marked. Robin Hood and his merry men all have American accents. The wicked Sheriff of Nottingham and his evil cronies speak with English accents.

Even Pontius Pilate and the Romans have English accents – unless like the famous centurion played by John Wayne they are due at some point in the film to be revealed as "goodies" after all.

Most people are on their guard when dealing with someone who has a "foreign" look – dress or accent markedly different from their own.

Similarly someone who does not match up to a pre-conceived notion of what they should look like can meet some initial reserve.

Most people expect their bank manager to "look like a bank manager". However much you believe that you have your prejudices under control you might well look askance at the bank manager (or accountant, doctor or lawyer) dressed in torn jeans and a dirty shirt and sporting pink hair. There would be immediate doubts that such a person could be relied upon to give the service you require.

These are, of course, extreme examples but the effect of appearance is there in more subtle differences.

Treat your prospect's desk as if it were part of his or her private house. Putting your feet on the desk is clearly unacceptable, but there are other less obvious pitfalls to avoid.

The answer is to conform to the industry norm and to leave the expressions of individualism for the weekends. Give the appearance that will, generally, please and make others comfortable in your presence.

A SMILE AND COURTESY

A smile and a courteous greeting are also emotional necessities. "Yes", you say, "that's obvious".

No doubt, but not all sales people remember it. Sales people *do* sometimes scowl or look glum.

They *do* sometimes forget to say "Good morning" to the audience.

Sales people will sometimes:

● Sit down before being invited to do so.

● Light a cigarette without checking that the customer has no objection.

● Move things on the customer's desk to make room for a briefcase or even (it has happened) stick their feet on the customer's desk.

All of this is a way of saying "I have no respect for you Mr Bloggs". At least Mr Bloggs may take it that way.

Presenters have been known to:
● Lean heavily on the lectern as if exhausted by the effort of presenting.

● Yawn and glance at the clock as if bored.

● Try to humiliate a member of the audience who asks a difficult question.

These are all ways of making the audience feel you have no respect for them. However, provided you have not made any such foolish mistakes, how do you make emotion work for you?

MAKING EMOTION WORK

People are not only more willing to buy from people who "look OK" but also from people who:

● They feel they can trust.

● Show friendship.

● Demonstrate integrity.

● Are credible and dependable.

● Have an aura of authority.

● Show commitment to satisfying the buyer.

● Show appreciation for the buyer's standing and reputation.

It is unlikely that all of these emotional factors can be brought into play at the very first meeting or presentation. Integrity for instance may be something to be demonstrated over a lengthy period of time and the salesperson may well plan the sales campaign as a series of presentations which gradually build up a rapport with the buyers. It is wholly unrealistic to believe that every member of the audience will instantly regard you as a helpful, friendly, honest and totally credible person – however much you smile or otherwise look the part.

Every opportunity to develop the buyers' sense of trust and belief in you must be taken. The following are some ways to achieve this goal:

● Never knowingly give buyers any incorrect information about the product, service or after-sales service. A deliberate lie is *not* the mark of a professional who, whatever his personal principles may be, will know that the chance of being found out is high and the buyers' trust in him will immediately disappear.

If, as can happen, incorrect information was given to the buyers by mistake then they must be informed of the error without delay. This corrective action should not be left out because of fears of looking incompetent or careless. The fact is that the great majority of people will appreciate your honesty in admitting a mistake and their trust in you will be increased.

● Be a nice guy. An English salesman spent over an hour explaining his service to an American audience. One particular prospect showed interest but was clearly not willing to commit himself to buying and the salesman decided that he would have to follow up with at least one personal visit if a sale were to be made. However, he had given a full presentation and knew that the service would be of positive benefit to his prospect. The salesman realized that any obstacles to a sale were probably emotional ones which would need time to overcome. By sheer chance the salesman met the prospect in the bar of his hotel that same evening.

The prospect, who was waiting for his wife, accepted the offer of a drink – the salesman having promised (with a smile) not to talk business. The conversation ranged over a number of topics and the prospect mentioned the love of his life – an elderly British car. It turned out that the prospect, despite difficulties in obtaining spares, enjoyed running the car and doing all the repairs and servicing himself.

Whether consciously or not, buyers are looking for eight qualities, aside from product reliability and price, and it is up to you to provide them.

He commented that what he really wanted was a repair manual. He had tried to find one without success. The salesman then offered to obtain one for him and explained that they were readily available in shops in England for a couple of pounds. The prospect was delighted and pressed five dollars into the salesman's hand.

The next morning there was a message for the salesman asking him to call on the prospect at his office. He did so and was told that having thought about it overnight the prospect had decided to buy the service. The salesman returned to England with an order and mailed the repair manual to his customer. He may have been wrong but the salesman was convinced that his friendly offer (with no strings attached) had won him the order.

Such *spontaneous* friendly acts can play a significant part in building a rapport with the customer. However, they *must* be sincere and not at all contrived. Contrived good turns are seen for what they are and normally earn nothing but contempt. This kind of situation is more apt to occur in a one-to-one presentation, but can arise with one or more individuals from a group.

A sense of friendship can also be encouraged by discovering interests which you have in common. Opportunities arise from time to time in a presentation to indulge in some small talk. Thus, when there is a break for coffee (or over lunch) encourage buyers to talk about themselves. Most people are pleased to talk about themselves and a polite question can result in valuable information. You may for instance find that a prospective buyer is a keen gardener and this may be one of your interests too. If so, you are

on to a goldmine. The fact is – based on the principle that we warm to people like ourselves – that a shared interest breaks down barriers and encourages friendly feelings. However, your own interest *must* be genuine, so don't pretend that you are fascinated by photography or crazy about rock climbing if you are not. A few questions will soon show you up as a fraud!

Think about this from your own viewpoint. Do you find it easier to deal with people who have similar interests or experiences? Shared experiences in the forces or past attendance at the same school or college are also examples of situations which will, at least unconsciously, make the buyer feel you are someone he can do business with.

● Integrity can be demonstrated in a number of ways. One is by politely declining to give buyers any information about other

Building trust and rapport takes time, and you should be prepared to go back to the customer several times if necessary. It is unwise to press for immediate decisions.

Building a relationship with your customer is essential. Always treat him as an individual, finding out what you have in common and how your product can help him.

customers who may be competitors. It is not unknown for buyers to ask questions such as "How much of this product do XYZ Ltd buy each month?" or "Which grade does ABC Ltd use?" There is a temptation to please buyers by giving them this information in the hope of gaining a sale. Resist the temptation – they may be glad of the information, but will now know that if they buy from you confidential information about their company will be at risk.

● Your credibility and dependability can be demonstrated by knowing your product well and keeping any promises made. The ability to answer the buyers' questions clearly and without hesitation shows that you know your stuff and can be depended on. If for example, you agree to provide more technical information or send a sample, *then do it* – and do it when you said you would.

● Whatever your status in your company may be the buyers must see that you have "authority". This is not only the authority to agree to discounts, special packaging or

deferred payment terms. It is the authority that comes from a calm and confidential "presence", by taking your time before answering questions and having the courage to say "I appreciate what you are asking for, but I need time to consider it. I will give you a ring on this point tomorrow".

In other words you are nobody's pushover, you have respect for yourself as well as the buyers and you don't do business off-the-cuff.

● Making sure that you know what the buyers' needs are – and making sure that they realize you know their requirements – will help convince them that you are committed to their satisfaction.

Ask questions yourself, take notes and *listen*. Don't interrupt buyers even if you are keen to move on to another subject. Make them feel that every word they say is important to you. That should not be difficult because it is true.

If at all in doubt about the buyers' needs and wishes it is important to double check. Buyers will appreciate it, especially if you make it clear what you are doing. For example: "Could we go back over your delivery requirement Mr Snooks? I want to be quite sure I have got it absolutely right".

● Everyone likes to feel important and nothing is more pleasing than to find someone who recognizes something that we are proud of achieving. Providing that the salesperson is *genuinely* impressed or appreciative of something a buyer has done, a mention of it can work wonders. Casual and *uncontrived* remarks such as these will help:

● "You must have as much experience of four-wheel-drive vehicles as any of us here".

● "Your article about oil consumption in *The Engineer* seems to have made quite an impression".

or

● "I would welcome your advice on..."

Such remarks will gain the favourable attention of the person to whom they are made and of the audience in general. In one

Your customer's requirements must be paramount. Make every effort to discover his needs and then find ways to make sure your product or service meets them.

real-life case a salesman dealing with a somewhat pompous client remarked that the growth in his business was most impressive – *and* the salesman trotted out the figures showing that he knew what he was talking about.

During a coffee break the client turned to a colleague who had been present and said "I do like doing business with that young man. He is so good at his job". This was another

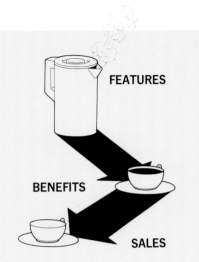

FEATURES

BENEFITS

SALES

Whether you are selling the toughest steel or the most beautiful paintings, always ask what your product will do for your customer.

way of saying "He thinks I am good at *my* job".

Above all, keep reminding yourself that you must work from the buyers' point of view. The people you are talking to are human beings too and their favourable attention will only be gained if you can make them *want* to listen. They do not *have to* listen.

Keep the emotional aspects always in mind and meet the buyers' personal needs in terms of their self-respect, sense of security and prestige.

The conscious, or unconscious feelings of buyers in the group will include:

● I am an important person and I want to be treated as such.

Failing to treat his question seriously enough can lose you customers.

● I want you to understand my view of things.
Show that you are concerned with his viewpoint .

● I want to be sure that what you are offering will be good for me.
The salesperson must demonstrate this.

● Is there a snag somewhere?
Give the full facts (warts and all).

● I must decide what to do.
The buyer must be helped and encouraged.

More will be said about these five aspects in the following pages as these techniques are developed further.

LOGIC

The logic-based satisfiers inherent in the product or service are those which can be demonstrated, seen or described. They are much more tangible than the emotional aspects, form the framework of the presentation and must be presented as benefits to buyers or their companies. They can include such things as:

> **CHECKLIST**
>
> ● Cost saving   ● Safety in use
> ● Reliability in use   ● Time saving
> ● Ease of use   ● Versatility
> ● Reduced administrative needs

Such benefits can be backed up with:

> **CHECKLIST**
>
> ● A sound maintenance service
> ● Prompt delivery
> ● Advice
> ● Secure packaging and clear labelling
> ● Easy-to-read instruction manuals

These benefits result from *features* of the product or service and must be pointed out to buyers. They must *not* be left to work benefits out for themselves because they may not be able to, or may not want to bother.

Some examples will illustrate the point.

A PRODUCT LIABILITY INSURANCE POLICY

You are offering insurance to cover the legislative liability of manufacturing companies which may result from defects in the product causing injury to a member of the general public.

Among the features of your policy there is a clause which states that the cover is worldwide and renewal notices are sent out automatically each year at least a month before the policy runs out.

These features can be translated into benefits like this:

● "Since the cover is worldwide (feature) you will not have to worry about accidents occurring overseas (benefit). You will not have to ask for endorsements every time you export your machines (benefit) or keep records of machines in other countries (benefit).

The automatic renewal reminders (feature) relieve you of the necessity to keep a note of the renewal date (benefit) and you will not find yourself without cover as a result of overlooking it (benefit)".

A PLASTIC

This time you are selling plastic granules which will be used by manufacturers of plastic bags, buckets, bowls and other items. Your product has some particular physical characteristics which represent substantial benefits:

● "This product has a density of 0.98 (feature) which means that anything made from it will be 20% tougher. This results in fewer customer complaints about cracking (benefit) and less wastage on the production line (benefit).

The constant viscosity (feature) makes moulding faster and increases output levels (benefit). In addition the special surfacing additive (feature) improves the polish on the finished article making it more attractive and increasing sales (benefit)".

It is the benefits which sell the product – features do not. However, the benefits which are mentioned in the presentation must be relevant to the buyers. There is no point at all in proudly pointing out benefits which are of no interest to them. If, in the insurance policy example, the companies present did no export business at all then the benefits from worldwide cover are valueless to them.

Benefits must be *selected* and offered with care.

At this point, it is important to mention another vital aspect – working out the benefits which will count. The true answer is not always obvious and if the relevant ones are submerged in a mass of irrelevant ones they will lose their impact.

WHICH BENEFITS ARE RELEVANT?

The most vital thing to recognize in choosing the benefits is that *companies* do not buy things. It is *people* who buy. This means that benefits which will make an impression must be benefits, directly or indirectly, to the human beings you are talking to.

This means that you must be able to decide what the needs and objectives of the individuals concerned may be. If, for example, you stress the cost saving aspects of the machine you are selling to a buyer who has no *personal* interest in the cost angle then you could be wasting your time. Such a buyer may, as the result of some bad experiences of machine breakdowns, be almost entirely concerned with reliability – especially if his

Anyone considering a product or a service is likely to have some doubts or fears and raise obstacles accordingly. Meet objections with benefits and further explanation.

boss has threatened to fire him if he doesn't find some dependable machines!

This means that not only do you need to have a sound knowledge of your product but you also need to think hard about the *people* you will be talking to. You may have quite a lot of information about them already or you may have to regard your presentation as a preliminary to a series of more specific one-to-one presentations to be made later. Alternatively the presentation may be structured to finding out or confirming the needs and objectives of the buyers in the earlier part and bringing out the relevant benefits in the second half.

This means some careful preparation which includes asking some questions:

● What are the personal objectives of buyers likely to be?

They might include desire to expand an empire, to be promoted, to reduce expenditure, to increase standing/prestige with colleagues or to please a difficult boss.

● What can be offered in the way of product features which can be translated into benefits which are likely to be personally meaningful to the buyers you are talking to?

● What doubts or objections might be raised? Remember that buyers will need to be convinced that the benefits offered are really there.

The most difficult case of all is when you have virtually no answers to these questions. In such circumstances you will need to find out as much as you can before the main part of your presentation. This means using that powerful tool of the salesperson's kit, the question. Don't be afraid to ask questions.

Providing they are courteously put and "open" (requiring more than a "yes" or "no" answer) most people will respond to them. If necessary, you can point out that you want to check some facts before going on *in order not to waste the buyers' time.* This should put them on your side because you are showing that you are trying to work from their viewpoint.

Listen carefully to the answers to your questions, weigh each person up as an individual and look out for any signs of problems they may have. If problems are mentioned zero in on them as these may be solvable by benefits which you can offer.

Watch out for any objectives which may be mentioned or alluded to. These might involve (apart from work problems to be solved):

● Ambitions and hopes for the future
● Obligations – personal and business
● Responsibilities – personal and business
● Fears
● Private interests.

If an objective is mentioned you can openly discuss it. However, do not discuss a suspected objective (this may embarrass the buyer) and only discuss one objective at a time. Discussing two or more objectives at once can become confusing for all parties. Any benefits you wish to mention should be related to the particular objective being discussed. The temptation to pour out all the benefits causes confusion and reduces their effect.

There is of course no magic formula for finding out what someone's objectives are. The requirement is for intelligent and sensitive questioning followed by patient listening combined with common sense.

However once you hit the right subject it is likely that you will obtain the information you require simply because people like to talk about what interests them.

THE IDEAL – A CHECKLIST

It is rarely possible in real life to know everything about a buyer which will help you to find their objectives and match them with benefits.

However, we need a target to aim at. The following is a checklist of topics to examine:

● Each buyer's position in the company hierarchy.
What level of responsibility and authority does he have? Does he make the buying decisions or does he need you to help him sell the product to his boss or someone else? His objectives may be to obtain that help and to show his boss how on the ball he is.

● The buyer's past experience and qualifications. This may indicate how sophisticated his objectives may be and how readily he can appreciate the value of the benefits offered to him.

● The politics of his organization. Is his company one of those hire and fire outfits where making a mistake is certain death? If so his objective could be to avoid taking any risks and to maintain a low profile. You may have to offer lots of back-up and after-sales service or benefits to suit this objective.

● Last, but by no means least, what the buyer's company does, its products, services and the market it competes in.
Many objectives will be concerned with satisfying the buying company's own customers, fighting off competitors or simply surviving in a tough environment. Your benefits must suit such needs.

YOUR "LOGICAL" IMAGE

We have already considered the personal aspects of the image that you present. Equally vital is the "logical image". This is made up of the characteristics which buyers will attribute to you during the course of your presentation. They will be influenced, favourably or otherwise by your experience and knowledge and the level of confidence they have in you.

Even the best of products is difficult to sell if the buyers doubt the knowledge of the salesperson or suspect that he has insufficient experience.

These doubts – and doubts about the product too – are often revealed by the questions that buyers ask. They may be direct and openly challenge your abilities but most people are more subtle. For example comments or questions such as these are warnings that a buyer needs some assurance:

"I find that rather surprising..."

"Are you quite sure about that...?"

"How often have you seen that happen...?"

"I am not sure that is quite right..."

The salesperson must respond to such remarks with a positive statement which settles any doubts.

For example:

"I worked out the answer to a very similar problem about five years ago..."
This shows that there *is* an answer to the problem *and* you have been around for some time.

"When I worked as a production engineer I found that…"
With a statement like this you are establishing your credentials.

"There is no doubt at all – I have seen this lubricant in use in at least four types of jet engine".
This is a statement designed to support claims for the product *and* show your breadth of experience.

"Let me demonstrate…"
A demonstration either of the product in action or even a calculation written out on a flip chart can remove doubts entirely.

Sometimes such reassuring statements are most effective when made some time after the salesperson *suspects* that a buyer has doubts. This is particularly the case when the suspicion is vague and there is a danger that the buyer will conclude that "the lady protests too much". A saleswoman in the insurance industry suspected that her prospect doubted her technical knowledge but that he was too polite to say so. On her way out of his office she pointed to some trade magazines which she had seen lying on a table in the reception area.
"Did you see my article on insurance for container thefts which I wrote last year?" she asked.
The buyer was visibly impressed and never showed doubts again.

Naturally, your product knowledge must be complete and up to date if buyers are not to have doubts about you. One aspect of this is the "Don't bother it's not important syndrome". This crops up in cases like the following:

BUYER "If I overload the electrical system will the machine cut out before any damage is done to the motor?"

SALESMAN "Oh, I think so…it should be here in the manual…somewhere…can I use your phone to ring my office?"

BUYER "Don't bother it's not important".

This statement is a serious warning that you have lost the sale. You have lost it

Knowing what the buyer's objectives are is fundamental to making a sale. This is not always easy as the buyer may not reveal them. However, it is usually possible to make some shrewd guesses and then confirm his true objectives by asking some subtle questions. The buyer's job, his seniority and his relationship with his boss can all offer clues, as will information about his company – from its politics to its products.

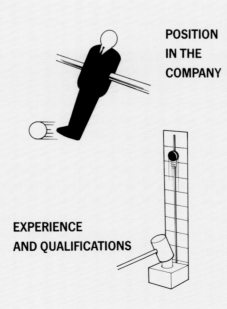
EXPERIENCE AND QUALIFICATIONS

POSITION IN THE COMPANY

COMPANY POLITICS

COMPANY'S ACTIVITIES

because you have damaged the buyer's confidence in you and not because the product was unsatisfactory.

The answer which should be forthcoming in such cases will be along the lines:

"Yes, definitely. There is an automatic cut-out which activates within four seconds of an overload".

The buyer in such cases is checking that the product actually works in the way he needs and will not cause him any problems. This is an entirely logical and reasonable action on his part and the salesperson must

If it's hard to describe, it's hard to understand. A visual or a demonstration will make your job easier and be more convincing.

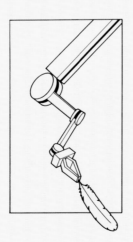

be able to respond to it. It is vital, therefore, that in preparing for a presentation, questions of a technical nature should be anticipated and the answers checked in advance.

RUNNING INTO DIFFICULTIES

Presentations are subject to a number of awkward situations. The interesting aspect about all these is that a question can solve every one of them – or put you on the right track to doing so.

There are five main problem areas which can face the salesperson from time to time:

● A buyer will not keep to the subject the salesperson wishes to discuss. Most of us are familiar with the member of the audience who raises and re-raises apparently irrelevant or trivial points.

The vital requirement is to be quite sure that what the buyer wants to talk about really is a waste of time before you do anything about it. The chances are that what he is interested in is important to him and you must look at it from his point of view. However, some buyers will drift off into subjects which have nothing whatsoever to do with you or the presentation.

It is essential to bring the subject back to the job in hand or you can find yourself wasting both your time and that of the others. A carefully worded question or a series of questions can bring the conversation round to the topic you want and will score points with the group.

For example:

"How do you find our billing system these days?" (You know it is working well).

"Oh, fine".

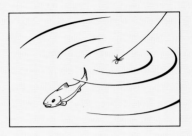

Red herrings are a waste of your time. If the presentation has drifted away from the subject, a well-phrased question can pull it back.

"That's good news, we have also recently improved our packaging..."
(This is the point you want to discuss.)

Take a lesson from the politicians being interviewed or in a discussion group on television. They are masters of the art of changing the subject by asking a question which shifts the whole discussion.

● A buyer appears to have the wrong idea.

Quite often a customer will have made an incorrect assumption or has been told something, perhaps about your product, which is incorrect. A salesman representing a major financial company was selling an insurance package. Suspecting that something was wrong he asked:

"Have you seen our figures for the return on investments?"

"No" said the buyer "but you boys keep

the investment earnings so it is of little interest to me".

The salesman had discovered the problem and was able to explain that all the investment earnings went to the clients and not to his company. He later found that the buyer had been misled by a broker offering a competitive product.

It is not a good idea to challenge a buyer or accuse him of being wrong, especially in a group presentation. A question however will open up the subject in a neutral way and allow you to provide the right information in a non-emotional and non-challenging way.

● The buyer thinks he has got all the facts – the salesperson knows he has not.

Once again the buyer must not be challenged or accused of ignorance. A question such as

"Have you seen the latest figures on oil consumption?"

or

"Would you like to see the test results?"

can open up a discussion in which the salesperson can provide additional information and, if the question is carefully phrased, give the buyer an alibi for not knowing it already. It might be easy for him to say that the latest oil consumption figures had not reached him (no doubt held up in the post-room) but very hard for him to say that he did not know them and had made a wild guess.

● The buyer is concealing his true feelings.
Some buyers will sit looking at the salesperson with a deadpan expression and say nothing – unless asked. Questions such as "How does this look to you?" or "Can you

see how the scheme will improve safety?" may well bring his feelings into the open.

The buyer may conceal his feelings simply because he is not sure that he has understood (and doesn't like to admit it) or is worried about some aspect of your product. If you suspect this is the case ask a question with an alibi such as "I have gone over it rather quickly Mr Bloggs. It is a bit difficult to take it all in at first go. Is there anything you would like me to explain further?" This question takes the pressure off the buyer. He can agree that you explained the service rather quickly and therefore *he* cannot be blamed for not fully understanding it. *Always* keep the members of the audience feeling comfortable.

Never humiliate or fight a customer. If you think he is wrong, blame yourself for any misunderstanding and then tactfully explain the facts as you see them.

Listen carefully to the answer to any question put to a buyer and listen carefully to any questions put to you in return. The buyer's questions can reveal a lot and may be prompted by all sorts of worries (not openly expressed) or a lack of knowledge which he finds embarrassing. Help him in such cases – never humiliate him.

● A self-imposed awkward situation.

Some sales people look upon a presentation as a kind of battle. Buyers are regarded (and treated) as enemies to be beaten. The adversarial attitude is wholly wrong and the salesperson who boasts "I screwed old Bloggs all right. Made him take an extra 20 tons and no discount. I showed him what", is asking for trouble. Old Bloggs will, if he realizes he has been screwed, do all he can to find another supplier and will have absolutely no friendly feelings towards the salesperson.

Selling should be a co-operative operation with give and take on questions of price, delivery and so on with a view to ending up with a result which pleases *both* parties. A few concessions (which can be traded for concessions from the buyer) can make all the difference. What is more if the buyer sees you as a co-operative person working with his viewpoint in mind he will come back to you for more.

Don't create your own awkward situations by being aggressive and pushy. Assertive and businesslike? Yes. That is something that buyers respect.

DEALING WITH OBSTACLES

In any sales situation there are actual or potential obstacles which the salesperson

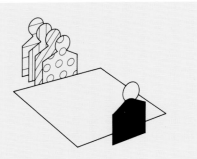

Not everyone wears his heart on his sleeve and the buyer may not be revealing his true feelings. Careful questions will help you to assess this.

may encounter and must overcome. There are ways and means to cope with them all – sometimes to a degree which turns an obstacle into an advantage – providing that the salesperson has done his homework and has benefits to offer.

There are eight common types of obstacle which can be briefly described as:

● HABIT This is exemplified by buyer's statements such as: "We have always done it this way" or "We have always purchased in monthly quantities".

● FEAR The fear obstacle is often caused by doubts which the buyer has about the product, the service or what may happen if he commits himself.

"I am not sure that a big company like yours will take much care with us. We are rather small".

● PRICE An unwillingness to spend the money or to make the effort.

● DETAIL "I am happy about this in principle but…

● COMPETITION "ABCD Ltd, are offering a very good deal".

Alternatively the buyer may simply be influenced by a desire to have a choice.

● PERSONALITY Rude, bad tempered, aggressive and haughty buyers.

● COMPLAINT "The last load you sent us was all the wrong colour, then your credit note was sent to the wrong office and it was for the wrong amount".

● LACK OF INFORMATION "I don't see why you people use shrinkwrapping…"

Sometimes the buyer has the wrong information and believes it.

In all these cases there is some part of the buyer's viewpoint which is at odds with the salesperson's ideas and objectives. To overcome an obstacle you must radically change the buyer's thoughts and perception.

The first step is to remove any emotion from the situation. This is a vital requirement and must be achieved *before* dealing with the obstacle.

It is not necessary to agree that the obstacle is a valid one but it is necessary to show understanding of the buyer's viewpoint and, possibly, express sympathy with it. The technique to be used is termed "fencing".

FENCING TO REMOVE EMOTION

Suppose that a member of the audience says "I expected you to start your presentation 20 minutes ago. We are busy people and if you want to do business with us you had better sharpen up".

Clearly the buyer is annoyed *and* his self-esteem has been punctured by the salesperson arriving late for the presentation. Suppose also that the salesperson had arrived on time but due to the barrier to the customer's own car park being stuck he had been unable to get in and thus lost 20 minutes finding another parking spot.

The *worst* response to the buyer would be to blame him or his company:

"I was here on time but your damned car park barrier was stuck and I had to mess about finding another place".

This response would immediately raise the emotional level – possibly adding embarrassment to the buyer's irritation and further aggravating the injury to his self-esteem.

A better answer (there is rarely one which is *exactly* right) would be:

"I am sorry Mr Bloggs (*apparently* accepting the blame), the last thing I wanted was to be late (restoring the buyer's self-esteem). *We* ran into a little problem today – it seems that the people who supplied *the* car park barrier have slipped up…(Placing the blame on a third party who is not involved in the discussion.)

Note that the salesperson says "*We* ran into a little problem…" not *I* ran into one. Using "we" shares the difficulty and removes the impression of two sides in a dispute. Similarly the salesperson refers to "the" car park barrier not "your" car park barrier. This also helps to neutralize the problem, whereas saying "*your* car park barrier" is close to blaming the buyer for the delay.

There are a whole range of emotion reducing expressions which the salesperson can use without actually accepting blame or responsibility.

For example:

"If I were in your position I would feel as you do...but..."

or

"That is a perfectly understandable conclusion..."

These expressions are particularly helpful when you know that the problem has been caused by the buyer himself.

The situation could be made even more difficult by bluntly making him aware that he is at fault and it is necessary to give him an "alibi" to save his face. Bear in mind that he may well come to realize that the fault is his and hopes that you do not realize it too. Make him feel that you do not realize it.

"Looks like another computer error." It can be helpful to shift the blame to a neutral person or thing. However, this tactic should be used with care as an alibi, not a lie.

Alibi-providers can include:

"It seems that I did not explain the discount system very clearly Miss Jones, would you like me to run through it again?"

"This looks like another one of the computer errors..."

Computers don't actually make mistakes but many people think they do. In addition, blaming the computer is a convenient way out of trouble and the computer will not argue about it.

"Not surprising in view of the bad weather we have been having lately..."

Blaming the weather can also shift responsibility to a neutral and silent "third party".

In most cases the buyer with uncomfortable guilt feelings will leap with glee at the alibi you provide and the emotional level will subside rapidly.

Skilful fencing can switch feelings of anger, resentment, irritation and the like to feelings of relief, friendliness, and so on. They are, after all, only different sides of the same coin.

THE HABIT OBSTACLE

In this situation the buyer has always done something in a particular way and the salesperson's idea means that he must make a change. Generally he has followed his old method simply because he has become accustomed to it and he adheres to it with little or no forethought.

"We have always used timber for our containers and they have always been all right".

The salesman must now remove, or avoid, any possible emotion by fencing.

"I agree that the timber containers have given good service (fencing) and I can understand your view. However, aluminium is much lighter and reduces lateral damage".

The sequence required is:

● Fence to avoid emotion.

● Repeat your idea – aluminium as a replacement for timber.

● Repeat the benefits of your idea so that, by coming last in the sequence, they are uppermost in the buyer's mind.

It is likely, by reminding the buyer of the benefits as the last step in the sequence, that further discussion will be on the benefits – which is exactly what the salesperson should try to provoke.

THE FEAR OBSTACLE

This obstacle can be created by the salesperson *or* a buyer either of whom can introduce feelings of uncertainty, doubt or anxiety which will interfere with the acceptance of the proposal.

Such feelings will be revealed by such statements as:

"I am afraid that the insurance costs will be too high for the volume of business".

"Your idea looks good on paper but I am not so sure that it will work out in practice".

"I am not sure that my accounts staff will be too happy about it".

"I doubt if my managing director will go along with this idea".

The salesperson should first deal with the obstacle by fencing to avoid emotion – not brushing aside the buyer's doubts. However foolish or ill-founded the fear may be, it is very real to the person who is feeling it and must be treated gently. Once again the salesperson must work from the buyer's viewpoint.

If the emotional level is low enough the salesperson must try to analyze, with the buyer, the factors which lie behind the sense of fear. For example, if the buyer is worried about the insurance cost, is this based on facts, such as actual quotations from an insurance company, or is it nothing more than a pessimistic assumption? Assumptions are common in business dealing and they are often wrong. People make them because it is easier than doing the work of finding out

the truth and like all "well known facts" assumptions should be treated with scepticism.

If the worry about insurance costs is based on an assumption the salesperson must provide the facts or offer to do so promptly – treat the buyer's expressed concern seriously however ridiculous it may seem.

Doubts that the idea will work out in practice must be examined in a similar way. The salesperson must gently probe the reason for the doubts and then deal with them sympathetically. If the doubts are well founded the salesperson should accept them and try to overcome them with benefits. Denying that there are any good reasons for doubt when it is clear that they exist will destroy the salesperson's credibility.

Expressed fears that the buyer's staff, colleagues or boss will not be happy about the salesperson's ideas can be tackled by offering help – after clarifying the reason for their anticipated objections. A common fear problem is that the accounts people (or someone somewhere) will have to change their systems or learn new ways to do things. This is a very real obstacle as none of us like change or having to work harder in order to learn new tricks – unless the benefits are too good to miss.

In such cases the salesperson can:

● Offer to explain the idea to the buyer's staff, colleagues or boss. This relieves him of the burden and at the same time means that he cannot be solely to blame if anything goes wrong later.

● Repeat the benefits, if they are strong enough, to give the buyer the courage to proceed.

Doubts expressed by the buyer must be examined carefully and sympathetically. Never brush reservations aside for they may be wellfounded.

● Translate the features of the product or service into benefits for the people (other than the buyer) who may be involved in various ways.

● Offer to organize any training required e.g. for machine operators who may be using a new raw material with different characteristics.

● Provide a VIP presentation to the managing director – and perhaps a visit to see the chief executive of a satisfied customer.

THE PRICE OBSTACLE

Price is not limited to the cash which will change hands. Quite often the cash is less significant to *the individual* you are dealing with than some other "cost" which means a great deal to him. Some aspects of this type of cost were mentioned in the fear obstacle but there are others such as the additional work that the buyer might have to do. If the buyer is say, the production engineer, he may say:

"We've always done it this way." Change can be worrying and the buyer may need reassurance. Never criticize his current methods.

"We would have to alter our machine settings to use this material".

or

"I will have to re-calculate all our running times".

Even if you are offering a price *reduction* there still may be an additional cost to the individual. The production engineer may be obliged to completely re-cost his operation and the cost to him may be many hours of midnight oil working out all the figures.

Any practical help which the salesperson can offer will help to reduce this sort of cost – again preceded with any necessary fencing:

"Yes, there will be some additional work in altering the settings (fencing) and I can arrange for one of our fitters to give you a hand..."

or

"Recalculating the operating cost is a problem. Suppose I give you some help with it? I could spend a couple of days with you next week..."

The offer of help may need to be backed up with the reminder of the benefits. In other words, you fully accept that the costs are real but not only will you give some help, the benefits make it all worthwhile. However, be sure that the benefits really are enough to make the cost worthwhile. A weak list of benefits can make your case worse. "Who are you kidding?" is likely to be the response.

In cases where the price obstacle is purely a matter of the cash which is involved, the salesperson must rely on the benefits. Cash obstacles will ideally be anticipated during the preparation stage and the value of the benefits worked out to enable the salesperson

to put the whole thing in perspective:

"Yes Ms Jones at 25p per kilo this additive is a penny a kilo more than you are paying now. We calculate that this will cost you an extra £1000 per month. However, this will be more than offset by savings in machine down-time and fuel costs. Having a look at these calculations..."

There is nothing to beat doing your homework, having the figures and demonstrating to the audience that you took the time to look at things from their viewpoint. A useful backing to this approach is to have ready a *true* story from a customer operating a similar machine. Providing you have permission from the customer to use his figures and facts (and this is made clear to the audience) these can be used in evidence to support your case:

"The Comfy Truss Company were also worried about the price – at first. These are

The buyer may be concerned about more than the price of the product. Help him to address associated problems such as retraining.

their latest figures which show a down-time reduction of 39%..."

Don't knock the opposition.

Buyers will often trot out an offer from one of your competitors at a lower price. There is always a temptation in these cases to point out some unsatisfactory aspect of the competitor's product or service. Don't – it does not make your product or service any better or more attractive.

Again some fencing may be needed to avoid any antagonism and then the benefits of your product stressed – not the deficiencies of the competitor or his product.

"Yes, Snooks computers are cheaper than ours and they have a good reputation. (Fencing *and* disarming the buyer with a tribute to the competitor.) The model I am describing to you has 20% more core storage capacity (feature of *your* product) which means that sorting and listing work is much faster (benefit)..."

Many sales have been lost by salespeople who sneer at the competition – often not being smart enough to realize that the buyer has been buying from them for years with complete satisfaction.

THE DETAIL OBSTACLE

Detail obstacles can also be termed "Hassle" obstacles. The service or product is wholly acceptable to the buyer but he is put-off by a relatively minor feature or features of your offer. These features are often administrative in nature and conflict with the customer's way of doing things or his particular situation.

Detail obstacles include such things as:

"Just a minor detail" can kill the sale. What may seem a trivial bureaucratic point to you can be a major obstacle to the buyer.

● Insurance company insistence on figures being provided in a way which the customer can only meet with a great deal of trouble due to the way they keep their records.

● Companies who prepare their invoices in a particular way which confuses the customer.

● Product coding systems which suit the convenience of the supplier but are a problem for the customer. In many cases these minor but irritating details are either "the way we have always done it" or based on the whim of the warehouse manager or someone else who has no contact with customers.

Looking at the problem from the buyer's viewpoint the salesperson must be prepared to negotiate the details – if necessary fighting a battle with his own colleagues to bring about changes which make it possible for the buyer to take the company's product.

There was a British company selling chemicals in Europe which was keen to obtain business from an important German company. The potential customer tested the products and liked them. They were satisfied with the price offered and there were no problems with the delivery arrangements. Everything looked set for a major contract to be signed when a detail raised its ugly head.

Sample quantities had been sent with the British company's standard label on each package. The German company asked for the information on the label to be printed direct on to the package itself as they found that labels could become detached, with resulting confusion in their warehouse or, worse, mis-identification of a product.

The salesman dealing with the customer said that this would be no problem. He promised to explain the customer's requirement to the distribution department and said he would write confirming matters when he sent the contract for signature. To the salesman's dismay the reaction of the distribution department was so negative that by the time he had persuaded them to change their ways (the warehouse foreman disliked change of any kind) the customer had placed an order elsewhere – with a supplier who could meet them on every point of detail.

This was one of those cases where the salesperson was on a hiding to nothing – a situation which can be avoided by an energetic sales manager and good internal liaison between sales, production and distribution.

THE COMPETITION OBSTACLE

It makes every kind of sense for a buyer to look at alternatives when choosing a supplier. When he does so you face the competition obstacle. The salesperson will deal with this situation more effectively if he realizes that it is natural for a buyer to wish to make comparisons and exercise choice. The salesperson should never get upset – quite the reverse. He might even agree that it is sensible for the buyer to make comparisons. Such a response at least gives the impression that he is not worried by the competition and has every confidence in his own product.

You must also face the fact that the competitive offer may be a better one for the customer. If so you can:

● Gracefully agree, leaving a friendly atmosphere as a good basis for trying again later.

or
● Look for a way to change your offer to make it the better one – subject to not being

Any buyer with sense will compare your offering with those of your competitors. Ensure that your presentation will enable the buyer to make a fair comparison.

Difficult personalities may be facing problems and need sympathy, although they may make your life tougher.

tempted into a sort of Dutch auction which leads to financial disaster.

or

● Restate your case to make sure that the buyer has a full appreciation of the benefits you are offering him. You may have failed to explain something sufficiently well.

Using questions can be very helpful in doing this and the obvious one is:

"What is it that particularly attracts you to Snook's products?"

He may tell you that it is Snook's payment terms – which you can easily match but have not so far said so.

There may also be habit or fear obstacles which have not emerged. Appropriate questions can reveal them and, having done so, the door is open for further explanation.

THE DIFFICULT PERSONALITY OBSTACLE

The difficult personality is the man who is short tempered, rude, arrogant, has a chip on his shoulder or knows it all.

The cause can be temporary or permanent and may include:

● Too much responsibility

● Fatigue

● Grief

● Shock

● Domestic worries

● Failure to achieve an objective

● Prestige worries

● Emotional immaturity

The salesperson faced with this living and breathing obstacle will be best placed to cope with the situation if he recognizes that in the vast majority of cases he should be sympathetic.

There are a few people who just seem to be born unpleasant. However there are not many like this. In most cases people who are difficult are struggling with a nasty problem and when the problem is solved will become normal and much easier to deal with. Giving the difficult personality the benefit of the doubt and adopting a sympathetic attitude (even if unspoken) will almost automatically lead the salesperson to deal with him in the best way.

The emphasis must be on the emotional "tools" described at the start of this chapter. The most powerful are:

● A polite and friendly manner.

● Making him feel good with a *sincere* compliment.

Your sympathy, patience and friendliness will not solve any background problem which he has but they can make it possible for you to deal with him.

If all your efforts fail and the emotional environment remains unfavourable, don't press on regardless as this will almost certainly make matters worse. Providing you remain polite, calm and firm it is likely that other members of the audience will feel sympathy for you. This could increase your chances of making sales to the others – a good reason for viewing the "awkward customer" as an opportunity rather than a problem.

A MORE DIFFICULT PROBLEM

A management consultant was in the course of presenting an idea for a training package to the administration from a rapidly growing company. The administration director, having listened in stony silence for a few minutes, suddenly burst out with some aggressive and uncomplimentary remarks about consultants in general and training packages in particular. The consultant, well experienced in selling, fielded the abuse with some skilled fencing and then decided to take a risk.

He launched into some tough comment of his own refuting everything that the director had said. This was done quietly but very firmly leaving the director in no doubt that his comments were regarded as ill-informed and not those of a professional manager. Instead of immediately being shown the door the consultant was treated to a broad grin from the director and the comment "I thought you might feel like that".

The meeting then continued in an ever more amicable way until a deal was concluded.

The consultant's instincts had told him that the director was not a genuine difficult personality but was either someone who enjoyed indulging in a little sadistic tormenting of the salesman or enjoyed a battle of wits and an argument.

He could, alternatively, have been one of those buyers who likes to pressure the salesman into a more hard hitting and convincing presentation. With a *lot* of experience some sales people develop an instinct for spotting these situations but take care, you are on dangerous ground.

THE COMPLAINTS OBSTACLE

The salesperson faces the complaints obstacle whenever a listener criticizes some action, plan, person or anything which affects him.

For example a member of the audience might say:
"The facsimile system you people use just doesn't work".

This type of complaint is one in which the buyer is stating a situation which he thinks needs correction.

He will feel that:

● He has suffered losses.

● The situation is unjust.

● The salesperson should appreciate his position.

● The salesperson should do something about it.
and:

He is concerned enough to make a fight over it.

Remember:

Any complaint is justified from the viewpoint of the person making the complaint.

To solve the problem it is necessary to obtain a clear and accurate understanding of the details (is it the facsimile machine, or the local telephone system, or is the customer using the wrong telephone number?).

While not necessarily accepting the blame on behalf of his company, the salesperson should show sympathy and concern and, above all, that he is taking it seriously.

If the buyer is at fault he must be given a

Never embarrass the buyer. You may rightly think he is stupid or ignorant, but making these feelings obvious will kill the sale. It is particularly important not to show him up in front of his colleagues.

face saving alibi ("I can quite understand how this happened – a very natural conclusion to come to...") and explain the correct way to do it.

At all events never leave the customer feeling aggrieved, disappointed or let down.

Complaints should be regarded as an opportunity to gain a good reputation with the customer and the other members of the audience. A quick solution and rapid action can produce more goodwill than a satisfactory service in the first place!

THE LACK OF INFORMATION OBSTACLE

This obstacle (often requiring much tact to deal with) arises when a customer will not accept your idea because he does not understand some aspect of it.

For example:

"I don't see why membership of the insurance scheme makes any difference".

or
"The government is not in favour of such schemes".
It is *vital* not to make the listener embarrassed by proving his ignorance in a blunt fashion and publicly humiliating him.

Once again action should start with fencing with the customer, taking the blame and then educating:

"We have discussed this with the Ministry of Trade and they have confirmed that providing...they are wholly in favour".

A statement such as this should regain the favourable attention of the buyer and it should be possible to restate your proposal and the benefits which are relevant to him.

CHECKLIST

A survey carried out among professional buyers included a question on what most annoyed them about sales people. The 10 most frequently mentioned complaints were

The salesperson:

• Does not have enough product knowledge to explain adequately.

• Is unable to show what the product can do for the buyers.

• Makes the presentation without regard for the needs of the buyers.

• Talks too much and listens too little.

• Uses "canned" sales talk.

• Makes a disorganized presentation.

• Assumes that the buyers know a lot more about the product and does not check this out.

• Repeats himself over and over.

• Brags about himself.

• Changes his story when it seems to be to his advantage.

Clear, relevant visuals, a confident, well-rehearsed sales talk, comfortable seating, and appropriate dress are all important ingredients in a successful presentation.

THE PREPARATION

The success of a presentation largely depends on planning, preparation and rehearsal. It is vital to consider every aspect — from the type of audience to the environment — before beginning to structure the presentation itself.

Before you begin to think about equipment or even about visuals, you will have to make several decisions which will have a vital bearing on the style and type of presentation that will be made. First you must decide what you are hoping to achieve, for this will set the whole tone of the event. It is also important to bear in mind just who will be in your audience so that you can pitch the level accordingly. Decisions on the information to be presented and how best to present it will reflect the type of audience you are addressing.

It is only when you have taken all these factors into consideration that you should begin thinking about where the presentation will be held, what information will be needed, whether you will need visuals and what kind of equipment is best suited to this particular occasion. Effective communication is the core of any presentation and thorough preparation is essential, particularly in a group presentation. Obtaining feedback and coping with awkward questions (and awkward questioners) will not only impress your audience (making that deal just a little easier to clinch), but give you the confidence to improve your next presentation.

WHAT ARE YOU HOPING TO ACHIEVE?

In other words, what is your objective? This goal should be clear in the mind of every person involved in the presentation. It will largely determine what you do and how you do it. There are a number of types of objective which you can choose including:

● INFORMING your audience – about, say, impending new products, service or back-up. You may, for example, be explaining to existing customers why you are replacing agencies in their part of the world with a direct

selling subsidiary. You will need to *reassure* customers that this change will not mean a reduction in service levels, but will produce benefits for them.

● PERSUADING a group, such as a trade association or similar body, to support you in a market study which could lead to the development of services which will benefit the association members.

● EDUCATING customers or agents in, say, the effects of recent legislation on how business must be conducted in future and *explaining* how your company will carry out its affairs to serve its customers best.

● SELLING your product or service to potential customers who do not know your company well (or at all).

● SELLING additional or new products or services to existing or former customers who already know your company.

The possibilities are many and the exact purpose will dominate the style and content of your presentation.

WHERE SHOULD THE PRESENTATION BE HELD?

Customers will need a very good reason to travel to your company training centre on the Isle of Skye – however delightful – and their convenience is what counts – not yours. *Other possibilities might be:*

● To hold the presentation at your factory so that the product can be demonstrated.

● To find an hotel with good conference

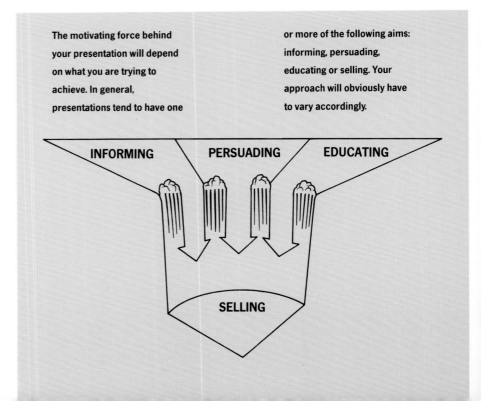

The motivating force behind your presentation will depend on what you are trying to achieve. In general, presentations tend to have one or more of the following aims: informing, persuading, educating or selling. Your approach will obviously have to vary accordingly.

INFORMING   PERSUADING   EDUCATING

SELLING

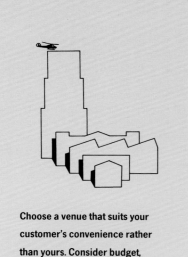

Choose a venue that suits your customer's convenience rather than yours. Consider budget, facilities and accessibility before making a choice.

facilities and good catering.

● If only one company is involved, to give the presentation on the customer's premises. This option may present problems if you need to use films, videos, etc., for which the customer has no facilities.

WHAT INFORMATION WILL BE NEEDED?

A failure to have the necessary facts and background information can lead to disaster. A presentation was made by a British company to the representatives of a number of Dutch companies selling a support service to companies in the transport industry. All went well until the time came for questions from the audience. The first questioner asked how the service fitted in with a local, legally-binding arrangement which governed many aspects of the way business could be done in the Dutch transport industry. The two men making the presentation could not answer the

Your choice of venue will be governed by the number of people, the equipment and the type of presentation. The hotel conference room (above) suits a formal presentation to a large audience. Hotel staff will be available to supply refreshments and other requirements. The smaller room (right) is suitable for a discussion-orientated presentation to a small group.

It is vital to research your audience. There is no point, for example, in delivering a highly technical scientific talk to general sales staff.

question for the simple reason that they had not obtained and studied a copy of the agreement. The credibility of the presenters promptly evaporated and not one customer was gained.

WHAT KIND OF PEOPLE WILL BE IN THE AUDIENCE?

Too many presenters limit this knowledge to the names of the people and their job titles. *Much more may be needed, such as:*

● Why each individual has been chosen to represent his company. (Is he a technical man selected to vet technical matters?)

● Which individuals will have decision-making authority and which are attending simply to report back to others in their

organization. The latter must not only be successfully convinced that your product or proposal is a good one, but they must also be motivated to sell it to their colleagues *and* be given the means to do so.

● Are there any people on the list with whom you have had problems before? Are they likely to ask awkward questions which will damage your reputation or credibility?

● Are there any people who might feel threatened by your proposals or be worried about them?

A firm of management consultants made a presentation to a company in London with the purpose of selling their services. Among the audience was an internal consultant who could see redundancy or (at best) reduction of his influence looming if the consultants were employed. He asked many difficult questions, mainly about cost, and successfully fended off the threat.

Had the consulting firm anticipated this reaction, they could have included in their presentation a clear statement that they:

● Would need and welcome the support of the internal consultant

● Would involve him in everything they did

and, possibly

● Would leave implementation of any changes resulting from their recommendations to him.

Such tactics would have reduced the probability of opposition and enhanced the chances of obtaining a contract. Instead, they responded aggressively to the internal consultant's questions and tried to diminish

his standing, which did not go down well with his colleagues.

WHAT, BY WHOM AND HOW?

Having dealt with the considerations above, the next step is to concentrate in some detail on what is to be transmitted, by whom and how.

Remember that what you say will depend on the result you want to achieve (educating, informing, selling, etc.) and what the viewpoint of the audience is likely to be. The likely thinking of the audience must be considered at some length, taking into account such factors as:

● The factual data they will want – costs, timing, training, distribution, guarantees, after-sales service, etc.

● The technical information needed. If the audience are engineers, chemists, designers or architects, their interests will be very different from a group of accountants, lawyers or administrators.

● What problems are likely to be in the minds of the audience? Are there any possible anxieties which your presentation can relieve (or make worse)?

● What are the objectives of the audience likely to be? What features of your product should be described, and which resulting benefits are relevant to the objectives of the participants.

For example, if the audience includes a production director, output rates or ease of maintenance may be the features of a machine which can give him benefits in the form of both convenience and meeting production targets. The accountant sitting next to him will be interested in the cost benefits derived from the same features.

In such a case, the presentation may include a statement such as:

"The demountable toggle-grommet (feature) reduces friction and eliminates the need for a specialist fitter.
This means that production staff will gain higher output levels and can use unskilled labour.
At the same time, this cuts costs per unit output and reduces maintenance charges – something the accountants will no doubt find attractive…"

NOTE: *Work at this stage should be aimed at producing a "core-message" – the full "script" with all the trimmings can be finalized later.*

Who makes the presentation is another vital factor, and the emotional needs of the audience must again be considered. Every member of the audience will want to be treated as a VIP (which they are!), so sending a junior salesman to talk to a roomful of directors may not go down too well. There are times when the Chairman or Chief Executive should be present, if only to make some opening remarks, and to perform a social

As a presenter, you should be thoroughly prepared, dressed appropriately and fully conversant with the equipment. It is also important to stand in a position which will not block anyone's view, to look at each member of the audience as you talk and to beware of irritating mannerisms.

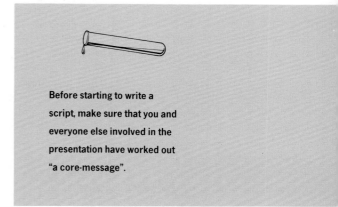

Before starting to write a script, make sure that you and everyone else involved in the presentation have worked out "a core-message".

function during the coffee break or lunch session. His presence adds weight to the occasion, and the effect is even better if your VIP plays a more active role by taking on some significant part of the presentation himself. Needless to say, your VIP must be a good speaker, know his stuff and be prepared to support your objectives.

One chairman, now retired, was a constant source of embarrassment to his colleagues. He insisted on taking the limelight at presentations, but treated each occasion as an exercise in personal promotion.

Audiences composed of middle level managers will be more at ease with speakers on a similar level to whom they can relate. Similarly, technical people can relate best to other technical people, administrators to administrators, and so on.

In summary, the people who should make a presentation are ideally:

● Appropriate to the status of the audience.

● Have an acceptable professional background.

● Have the ability to address an audience effectively.

● Know their subject inside out.

How the presentation is to be made should take into account:

● The opening stages – Big Bang or Softly, Softly?

● The sequence of the story which will have the most impact.

● Illustrations and other visual aids which will improve assimilation.

● The speed of transmission and general style: fast, slick, hard sell or slow, low profile and soft sell.

● Duration and breaks for rest and refreshment.

● Maintaining interest and reducing fatigue.

● Obtaining feedback.

● The closing stages.

The audience's body language can give you a good indication of their reactions to the presentation. With a large group, you may only be aware of those nearest to you, but with a small group you should be conscious of the atmosphere – alert and interested, boredom with attention beginning to wander, lethargic or questioning.

People respond to pictures with interest and remember them better than words. However, your visual must be relevant or it will distract.

THE OPENING STAGES

You will already have ensured that every member of the audience has been personally greeted, offered refreshments (if appropriate) and shown to a seat. These courtesies – designed to make sure everyone feels both welcome and important – should be reinforced in your opening remarks, which should include a welcoming statement and a word of thanks for sparing the time to attend the presentation. This can be followed by introducing the speakers with a brief description of each one. The description should, in low key fashion, establish the credentials of the speakers to remove any doubts which the audience may have about their qualifications or experience. An introduction such as "This is Fred Filbert our colleague from the production division" says too little.

A more effective statement would be "...Fred Filbert is our chief designer. As some of you may know, he is the man who led the team which developed the successful computer controlled welding machine. He has been with us for five years and was previously a leading light in the team researching surface properties at the University of London..."

Next, the purpose of the presentation should be explained. The presenter must not assume that everyone knows and understands why they are there. People sometimes turn up at presentations with a false impression of its aim. Even if everyone has the right idea, repeating it focuses the minds of the audience on the subject, re-directing their thinking away from any distractions which may be occupying them.

The next step is to tell them something about the format of the presentation so that they know what to expect. The duration, breaks for coffee, films or demonstrations can all be mentioned.

Finally, the audience can be invited to participate and ask questions at any time – if that is how you want to play it. You may prefer to keep questions until the end of each part of the presentation or until the whole programme has been completed. Questions as you go along can disrupt the flow and lead presenters off the track, but it is important to ensure that everyone is still with you. A useful compromise might be to stop at suitable points in the presentation, such as before changing subjects, and invite questions before continuing.

THE VISUALS

It is an old saying, and a true one, that a picture is worth a thousand words. Anything that can be made more clear more easily and more quickly with a picture, diagram or graphic should be identified (see pp54-9). People also respond well to things that they can touch and handle, so a few samples of a product which the audience can examine (see pp64-5) may be helpful.

SPEED AND STYLE

The question to ask is "What will the audience want?"

Sales people tend to enjoy the fast moving, high impact type of presentation; most others prefer something more sedate. A salesman presenting a Microfilm system to a group of lawyers came unstuck because he went too fast and made claims for the product which were too dramatic. All the claims he made were true, but he expressed them in terms which were overpowering for his audience.

Bear in mind that audience reaction varies from one nationality to another. A slick,

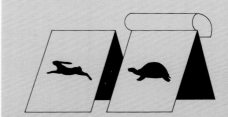

Deciding whether to give a slick, fast-moving performance or a simple, lowkey talk will largely depend on the make-up of the audience.

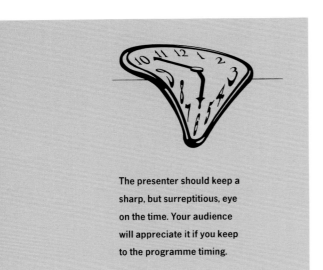

The presenter should keep a sharp, but surreptitious, eye on the time. Your audience will appreciate it if you keep to the programme timing.

"flashing lights" approach may go down well in New York, but could be over the top in Hamburg. In addition, foreign audiences may have difficulties with the language, so a slower delivery may be needed. Colloquial expressions may also have to be avoided when speaking to foreign audiences. Expressions such as "the bottom line" or "up front" are rarely taught in foreign schools and universities.

DURATION AND BREAKS

Few people can absorb information for more than 40 minutes. Fatigue and boredom set in with increasing effect after 30 minutes or so without a break. This does not necessarily mean a complete cessation of the presentation – like a coffee break – it could be a change of speaker, a short discussion involving the audience, questions from the

audience, a demonstration or anything significantly different from a continuation of a talk.

The events which can provide such a break should be listed so that they can be slotted into the programme. They must of course appear in logical places in the sequence, but they will serve to revive the interest of the audience after a "run" of listening.

OBTAINING FEEDBACK

If your audience falls asleep or walks out, you have obtained some feedback of the most unwelcome kind. Most people will stop short of such drastic action however and may just sit and show little or no reaction of any kind. A way of obtaining feedback which goes beyond looking at facial expressions is essential – important though that is. One way to get reactions is to ask the audience questions. Presenters are sometimes afraid to do this but it is often the best way to obtain information which would otherwise remain unspoken. Questions also help to involve the audience and reduce fatigue.

Have some questions ready on subjects such as:

● How members of the audience see themselves using the product.

● How they deal with the current situations.

● Which features/benefits they find most attractive.

The responses – even unwelcome ones – will provide valuable information and can guide the presenter as to what emphasis needs to be placed on various topics in the programme or whether something needs to be explained again or in more detail.

THE CLOSING STAGES

It is an interesting (and valuable) fact that audience interest goes up as the end of a presentation approaches. Any fatigue (or even boredom) which may have set in starts to fade away as people realize that the end is close and they will not have to listen and concentrate much longer.

This fact can be put to good use by pointing out that there are only a few minutes left. Having done so provides a good opportunity to summarize the presentation briefly, bringing out the main points and repeating the benefits which seem to have had most effect on the audience. For example:

"You have seen how the product reduces maintenance costs and speeds up production cycles. The back-up in the form of local service teams and a guaranteed

It is important to obtain some feedback from your audience. Allow time for questions or discussion either during or at the end of the session.

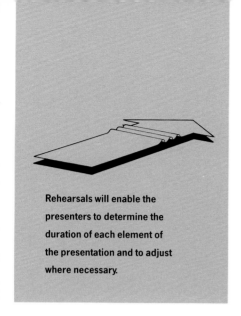

Rehearsals will enable the presenters to determine the duration of each element of the presentation and to adjust where necessary.

same-day response provides a level of security..."

Finally, a few words should be used to thank the audience for listening and to express the hope that the presentation was both entertaining and informative.

WHERE HAVE YOU GOT TO SO FAR?

You have now considered:

- Where to hold the presentation
- The objective
- The information you need
- The type of people you are presenting to
- What needs to be said – at least in outline
- Who should make the presentation
- How it should be done (in broad terms).

The next step is to produce a detailed scheme which involves a script (or scripts) (see pp50-1) and a detailed sequence. A helpful tool in this process is a storyboard (see pp50-1).

Once the scripts have been written and the visual aids/demonstrations prepared (see pp54-9), the penultimate item of preparation can begin. This is the rehearsal.

THE REHEARSAL

Rehearsing can begin by reading through the script several times and committing at least the gist of it to memory. Then, each speaker can work independently, practising his speech out loud. This can be done in the car on the way to work, in the bath or anywhere else which is private. The aim should be to acquire fluency through familiarity, but *not* to end up with a parrot-fashion recitation of something learned by heart.

Once a reasonable level of fluency and confidence has been acquired, the presentation team can hold a full scale dress rehearsal. This rehearsal will point out any weak element such as:

- Sequence faults.

- Duration problems.

- Visual aids which are not as effective as they should be.

- "Fumble factors" – the point at which, say, the speaker discovers that he cannot reach the projector switch without falling over his chair.

- The need for more "evidence" or information.

Ideally, a video recording should be made so that each participant can see his own performance. This can be a sobering experience even for experienced speakers, but it is better to spot one's own distracting habit of scratching the end of the nose (or

worse) every few seconds than to have the audience spot it. An additional "longstop" is provided by holding a rehearsal in front of an audience of colleagues who are primed to look for faults. This audience will enjoy finding the faults, and the presenters will discover better ways to tackle the job.

A major purpose of the rehearsals is to gain self-confidence. Nothing beats going into battle knowing that you have the subject at your fingertips and knowing how much time you have for each subject, exactly when to switch on the projector, etc. A high level of confidence not only results in a more convincing presentation; it also makes presenting a pleasure rather than an ordeal.

CHECKING THE CONFERENCE ROOM

Unless the presentation is being made on your own premises, you may need to

Live rehearsals will reveal any flaws in the visual aids, as well as the presenter's ability to operate the equipment efficiently.

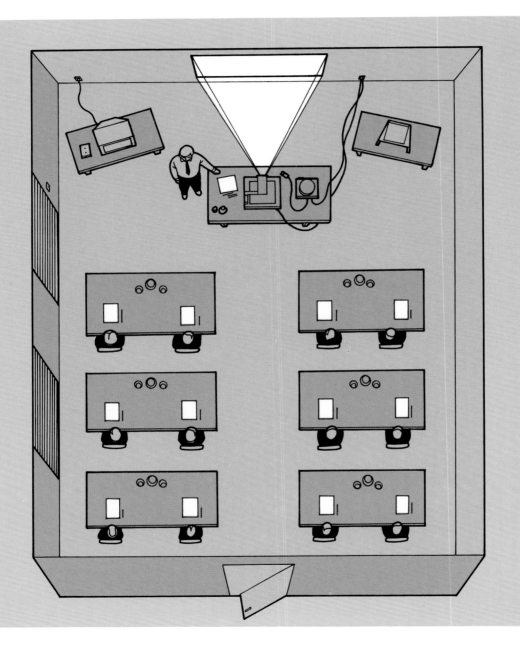

CHECKLIST

● Check projector distance from screen, and make sure that everyone will be able to see the visuals clearly.

● Check audience is not more than six times the width of the projected image from the screen.

● If you are using microphones, check that they are working and that people sitting at the back will be able to hear.

● Check that your visuals are in order, and the right way up.

● Familiarize yourself with the layout of the sockets and light switches.

● Check that you have the right number of tables and chairs.

● Check that any handouts or speaker support material are either on the desks or ready to hand.

● If you are providing water or soft drinks, make sure there are enough glasses and jugs or bottles.

● Make sure temperature and air supply are at comfortable levels.

familiarize yourself with the layout and the facilities. It will in any case be necessary to double check everything in the conference room:

● That all the power points work.

● That the video player or projector works and that you know which switch does what.

● That curtains can be opened or closed if necessary.

● That the projector screen is in the right place.

It is a good precaution to arrive at least an hour before kick-off to check such points as these and to bring a "survival kit" with you. The kit should contain:

● Spare bulbs and fuses for the projector.

● Spare felt tip pens for the flip chart.

● Extension leads in case the power points are in awkward places.

● A roll of insulation tape and an electrical screwdriver.

● Sticky tape, scissors, drawing pins, string, etc.

The Boy Scout's motto – Be Prepared – is one worth adopting!

If you fail to bring your survival kit, Murphy's law will take over. A fuse will blow, a power point will be dead and a paper chart will tear – five minutes before the first guest arrives.

PUTTING IT OVER

If your presentation has been thoroughly rehearsed, you should have eliminated most of the faults which may otherwise be part of your style of delivery. Good delivery can only come with practice, but there are a number of basic tips which will help:

● Take your time. There is a tendency for nervous speakers to gabble. Check yourself every few minutes, but don't slow down to a ponderous speed. This will make your words sound boring or pompous – or both. A *natural* speed – as if you were talking to a group of friends in your own home – is the ideal.

● Look at individuals throughout the whole audience – not at one or two people only or at the floor, the ceiling, the walls or your hands. Eye contact is an important part of communicating and helps to hold the attention of the audience.

● Avoid over-use of your favourite phrases. Constant repetition of "You see what I mean" or "The main point is..." can drive the audience crazy. Eventually some of them will begin counting how many times you use your pet expression instead of assimilating your message.

● Avoid talking in a monotone. Changing your tone of voice as appropriate to the text keeps the subject interesting and gives "life" to your presentation. A common fault is dropping the voice at the end of each sentence. This gives the impression (over and over) that the presentation has come to an end. The pitch should be maintained until a distinct part of a talk has finished or the whole talk has been completed.

There is, in addition, a particular hazard which presenters must watch out for – problem questions. As far as possible, these perils should be anticipated and the answers sorted out in the rehearsal. However, even the best-prepared presenter can find himself in difficulty. Then technique is needed to maintain control. The awkward question can frequently be turned into a positive advantage if the presenter has done his homework and has some benefits to offer.

Pace yourself. Nervous speakers are apt to talk too quickly. Remember to look at the audience, change your tone of voice and avoid mannerisms.

THE AGGRESSIVE QUESTION

These can come in many forms and for many reasons. For example:

● "What makes you think that your service is appropriate to my Far Eastern operation?"

Here the questioner, who looks after the Far

East, feels that you are claiming greater knowledge of the market than he has – and wants to let everyone know that *he* is the expert.

This situation should be handled by fencing and publicly restoring the questioner's prestige and standing as an expert.

"You are of course the best judge of that, Mr Green. I don't pretend to be an expert on the Far Eastern market, whereas you undoubtedly are. I hope that the facts and figures which we have given you will be convincing, but if there is any particular aspect you would like further information on..."

The last few words are designed to encourage the questioner to ask another question on a matter of fact – getting him away from a general attack, having

Questions should be viewed in a positive light rather than with apprehension. If you are well prepared, they are a good way of obtaining feedback.

acknowledged his superior experience.

● "Why have you skated over the legal aspects?"

This type of question normally indicates a member of the audience who has a *particular* interest in a *particular* subject. The "average" member of the audience is probably satisfied with the information already given.

Again, some fencing is required with a clear offer to deal with the subject in full if required.

"I am sorry if I have not given you as much information as you need, Mr White. It was not my intention to neglect the subject in any way. If there is any particular legal point which you would like to discuss – product liability perhaps?"

Once again, a return question is used to focus on a specific topic which, unlike a generalization, can be dealt with effectively.

Alternatively, you can ask if other members of the audience have similar queries – write them on a flip chart and deal with them one by one. If the audience as a whole is not interested, then an offer can be made to discuss the legal angles with the questioner immediately after the session. At all costs, you must *not* be seen to be ducking the issue.

THE SHOW-OFF QUESTION

Here the questioner is simply displaying his superior knowledge or cleverness to all and sundry.

Whatever you do, don't knock him off his pedestal. Acknowledge the expertise of the questioner and he will be your friend for life. However, you must not allow the question to leave you looking at a loss or defeated.

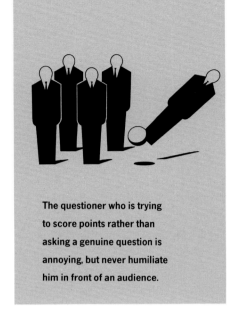

The questioner who is trying to score points rather than asking a genuine question is annoying, but never humiliate him in front of an audience.

A presenter at a seminar in Montreal was faced with the show-off problem when a member of the audience asked a long, complicated and very technical question clearly designed to display his great breadth of knowledge. The presenter's answer was along these lines:

"Boy, oh, boy, (with a smile) you have floored me there, Mr Clever. I would need some time to work out the answer to your question – as you will appreciate, your experience in some of the points you raise is greater than mine. Could we talk about it afterwards and take the question a piece at a time?"

The feedback obtained later from various members of the audience was highly favourable to this response since, as is almost always the case, everyone realized it was a show-off question and an answer was not really wanted.

THE OBSTACLE QUESTION

Some questions are actually expressing, more or less clearly, an obstacle.

"Does this mean re-training all our fitters?" (Price obstacle).

or

"Will we have to re-tool during the holiday period?" (Time obstacle).

or

"What about spare parts delivery on weekends?" (Detail obstacle).

Such questions need to be dealt with by re-stating the benefits to show that the price is worthwhile, and information must be given to clear up detail worries.

These are some of the awkward questions which may be thrown at you. There may be others, depending on the audience, the subject and other circumstances. A general guide to dealing with the unexpected curve ball is:

● Fence to reduce emotion and avoid becoming emotional yourself.

● If you don't know the answer, say so. You can offer the question to the audience and ask if anyone knows the answer. If someone provides it, thank them and move on.

● If you are unsure, put the question up for general discussion. This at least gives you time to make up your mind and/or to summarize the discussion into *your own* answer to the question.

"...I think that answers your question, Sir. High temperatures generally assist the process, providing humidity is below 80% or so..."

● Enlist the help of an expert colleague (if one is present) or the aid of a member of the audience who is an acknowledged expert. This will *not* reduce your credibility, but will demonstrate that you have the sense to call on the skills of experts — and that keeps the audience with you.

THE GOLDEN RULE – REMEMBER WHAT THE OTHER PERSON WANTS

The other person's viewpoint has been mentioned over and over and cannot be stressed too much. The thing that counts is what is in the mind of the prospect or customer, and you *must* work from that basis.

On the right is a list of what the *personal* needs of your listeners may be. These "wants" are normal, human and apply to us all. The professional salesperson will remember them and meet them — and improve sales results by doing so (benefit!).

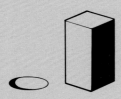

Some questions are prompted by concern about timing, price or some other problem. Be on the alert for unexpressed worries and provide reassurance.

CHECKLIST

● They want to feel that they have done a good job.

● They want to avoid future troubles.

● They want to be recognized by their superiors and others as people of good judgement.

● They want to keep their jobs and perhaps be promoted.

● They want their work to be easier.

● They want to feel that what they are doing matters.

● They want to avoid the insecurity that comes from surprises or changes.

● They want to count on you, now and in the future.

● They want to be listened to.

● They want a good explanation.

● They want to be liked.

● They want to finish negotiations and move on to other things.

● They want to know the truth.

● They want to be thought of as honest, fair, kind, responsible and important.

9.00 COFFEE/REGISTRATION
NAME TAGS

PHYSICAL CHARACTERISTICS
EMOTIONAL CHARACTERISTICS

9.15 WELCOME ADDRESS
BY THE CHAIRMAN.

STRONGER BRAND
5 CHARACTERISTICS

9.25 INTRODUCTION OF
FIRST SPEAKER BY THE
CHAIRMAN.

10.30 QUESTION TIME.

COVER LOGO - PERSONALITY
PHYSICAL / EMOTIONAL

10.45 COFFEE BREAK.

COMMUNICATE TO THE
CUSTOMER, CONSISTENT
PRESENTATION

11.00 PRESENTATION ON
CORPORATE IDENTITY

BRAND PERSONALITY
UPDATING.

WHAT IS CORPORATE IDENTITY?
HOW DOES IT COME ACROSS TO
STAFF / CUSTOMERS!

USING A STORYBOARD

This device – a piece of hardboard about 3ft × 2ft will do – is a cheap and effective way to get your presentation in order and provide the basis for scripts.

The storyboard is used to illustrate the sequence of events by sticking small squares of card or paper (self-adhesive notes are ideal) to it. Each note refers to a specific part of the presentation. The result could be cards showing respectively:

- Opening remarks

- Explanation of widget-driver

- Demonstration of widget-driver in use

- Audience invited to try the widget-driver

- Summary of benefits of widget-driver

- Coffee break

- Brief reminder of benefits of widget-driver

- Discount terms for bulk purchases

and so on.

The cards will not only help you get the sequence right, but will also help to avoid leaving something out – a real hazard if the subject is complex.

The cards can also show who will be handling the subject concerned and an estimate of the length of time required. The team preparing the presentation will find it helpful to construct the storyboard together – moving the cards around to find the best sequence. Noting the expected time for each part of the presentation on the cards also enables the team to keep themselves aware of the *total* time required and, if necessary, shorten or lengthen the time for each part. If

01-MAY-1990 17:56   T.B.S. COLOUR SLIDES   0273 23622   P.02

SALES CONFERENCE PRESENTATION - IDEM BRAND IDENTITY

SLIDE 1 *TITLE*

I'd like to talk to you this morning about brand identity. Let's start with an old friend.

SLIDE 2 *LOGO*

The current IDEM logo. Four letters that instantly trigger a whole chain of thoughts and associations in your minds and in the minds of your customers all over Europe and indeed the world. Thanks to sustained effort in every area of our operation to maintain and indeed improve a superb product, the principal characteristic a customer associates with those letters is of a brand of carbonless paper of the very highest quality. And, at a very general level, branding is indeed a means of differentiating one product from another.

SLIDE 3

That's how the Oxford Dictionary puts it. But if one analyses the key elements that go to make a successful brand in todays highly competitive market place, it becomes clear that there's a lot more to the whole business of branding than that simple definition suggests.

Self-adhesive Post-it pads are ideal for planning a presentation on storyboard (left). Visuals should be indicated on the script (above). Ideally, this should be condensed down to key words on index cards (right).

time is short, it may be necessary to cut out or shorten one or more of the parts or, conversely, allow more time for a demonstration or question session.

PREPARING THE SCRIPT

Some people find a written script (even if it will not be used at the presentation itself) the only way to put together a coherent and convincing talk. Some, perhaps people who are very familiar with the subject, may need only an outline of their piece. Others will use just a series of headings.

The storyboard can act as a guide to make sure that what is said does not duplicate something already covered or to avoid talking about a subject which will be meaningless until some other topic has been introduced. The script (or outline) should be marked to show where a visual aid will be used. This helps to avoid forgetting to show a slide or pass out a brochure.

MIND MAPS

A storyboard is not the only technique you can use to plan a presentation or write a script. Mind mapping, a technique developed by Tony Buzan, is a creative and highly effective means of preparing a speech or presentation. Most people are trained to use outlines and lists when planning a speech or a piece of writing. Hours of time and endless pieces of paper can be wasted as you attempt to develop and structure ideas simultaneously. Often the result is writer's block, ideas which are cut off before they lead anywhere, crossings-out, arrows indicating that various ideas are in the wrong place on your list, and feelings of frustration as you crumple up your outline and start again.

Mind maps, on the other hand, mean that you can let your ideas flow freely, with one association leading to another. Once you have written down every possible idea that comes to mind. you will immediately see patterns and connections which will enable you to organize your ideas into a logical sequence.

The process of using a mind map to write a speech or an article divides into two stages:

- Generating ideas. Let your mind wander freely. Put down anything which occurs to you, even though you might think it irrelevant at the time.

- Organizing your ideas. Examine your map analytically. This is the stage when you can cross out concepts which now appear irrelevant, highlight or number those which are linked, order points into an outline or make a second, more structured mind map.

Steps in developing a mind map:

- Draw a picture of your topic in the centre of a large piece of white paper. Pictures, however badly drawn, are easier to remember than words and will be more effective than words as a starting signal to your brain.

- Radiate out from your central picture using key words rather than sentences and lines which link the relevant key words together.

- Print your key words. This makes them easier to read and remember.

- Use colours for emphasis or to indicate relationships between key words in different areas of the mind map.

- Add images wherever possible as they will stimulate your creativity and help you to memorize key concepts.

- Arrows or shapes (circles, squares, triangles around words) can be used to show relationships between concepts and to help you organize your map.

MEMORIZING A TALK

Mind maps are not only useful for preparing a talk, they are a helpful aid or even a substitute for index cards when giving your presentation. Images, colours and key words are all easier to remember than an outline with numbered points. When you have finalized your speech, make it into a mind map again (or use your original map). Now put it away, take a blank sheet of paper and try to recreate your map. Check the result against your original and fill in any gaps. After doing this several times you will find that you can shut your eyes and recreate the map in your mind.

You may feel more confident if you carry index cards with your key points written upon them as a back up, but you may be surprised at how little you need to rely upon them if you have followed all the steps listed above.

MIND MAPS IN A PRESENTATION

Mind maps can be used effectively during a presentation, provided you explain briefly to your audience how they work. Using a flip chart or an overhead projector, you can gradually build up a mind map of your key points as you talk. This will not only hold the audience's attention, but will help them to remember what you have said.

Once you are familiar with mind mapping techniques, you will find that they can be used in all walks of life, from planning a holiday to solving problems to creating visuals.

This mind map on introducing computerized stock control is designed to illustrate the basic approach. However, everyone will have a slightly different approach.

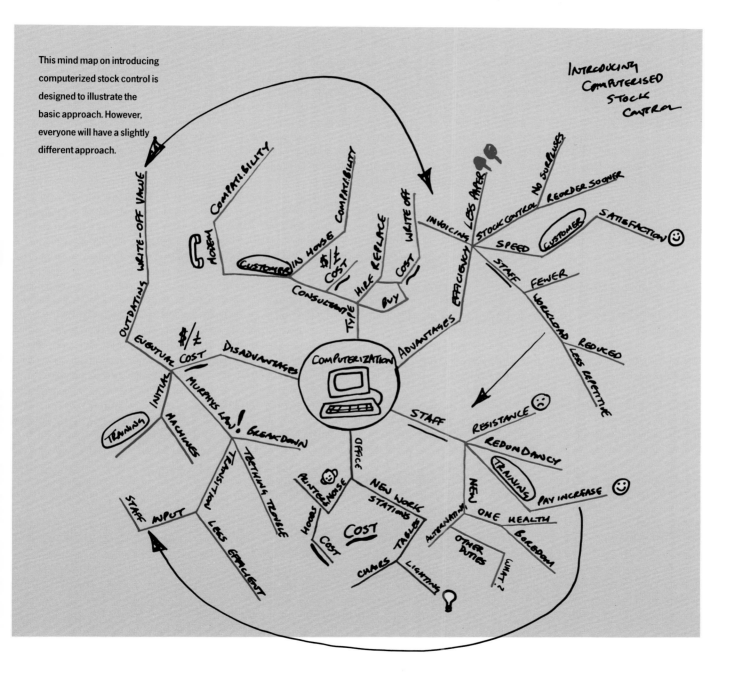

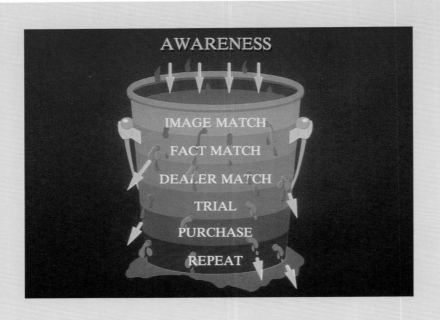

A single graphic image can
encapsulate a complex
situation. A strong concept,
clear labelling and an
effective use of colour give
this slide immediate impact.

- Do your visuals reinforce the corporate
image of your company?

- Will they look professional? Rough visuals
may be appropriate for a flip chart, but the
more sophisticated the technique, the more
essential it is to call in the professionals.

THE IMPORTANCE OF VISUALS

Using visuals in a presentation brings two
major benefits:

- When planning your presentation, it is
helpful to structure the information around
visuals. During the presentation itself a
sequence of visuals means that the presenter
has to cover the points relevant to each visual,
thus keeping the presentation on course.

- Research has shown that when words
alone are used, only 10 per cent of the
message is retained by the audience.
However, when visuals are added, retention
improves to approximately 50 per cent.
Another study has shown that computer-
generated graphics can make a presentation
43 per cent more persuasive.

CHOOSING THE VISUALS

Your choice of visual will be affected by
factors such as your budget, the equipment
you plan to use and the purpose of the
presentation. Graphically visuals divide into
five basic categories:

- Photographic images.

- Typography.

- Artwork.

- Charts and figures.

- Three-dimensional models.

VISUALS

The adage "a picture is worth a thousand
words" is particularly true when giving
presentations. However, the visuals must be
relevant or they will lose impact and distract
the audience, diluting your message in the
process. When planning your visuals always
keep the following points in mind:

- Does the method match the information?
(For example, an elaborate chart full of

figures would be inappropriate in a video –
the audience would be unable to assimilate
the information and it would slow down the
pace of the narrative.)

- Are the images relevant to the presentation?

- Is the information clearly and simply
presented? (It is better to show two separate
charts, each making a particular point, rather
than one complex chart which runs the risk of
confusing the audience.)

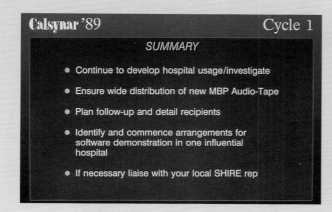

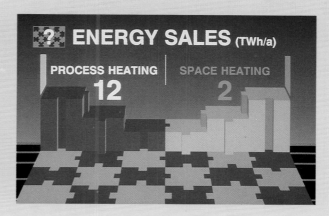

These four slides illustrate some points which you should bear in mind when briefing a designer, assessing roughs submitted for approval, or creating your own visuals. Clear typographic styling on a simple colour ground (top left) makes this visual easy to read and assimilate; enhancing an image (bottom left) can give drama to an ordinary subject; the company logo can be "animated" (bottom right); a complex design with little colour contrast may fail to communicate effectively (top right).

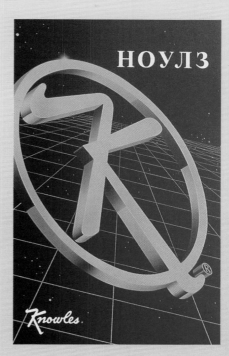

THE PREPARATION

PHOTOGRAPHIC IMAGES

Photographic images are a vital ingredient of most presentations, whether in the form of a slide (from overhead to computer-generated), a video or a handout. Whether produced professionally or in-house, they can be instantly effective, are flexible and, with today's technological resources, quick and easy to prepare.

TYPOGRAPHY

Typographic visuals vary from the rough and ready (the flipchart) to the sophisticated (computer-generated graphics). Your choice of typeface, background, colour and size will all influence the impact made by the visual on the audience. A professional graphic designer should be able to advise you on the most effective combination for your particular purpose.

56

ARTWORK

Drawings can often be more effective than photography in helping an audience grasp a particular detail, relationship or concept. Cartoons can capture an idea or a feeling in a way that a camera will not, but you should treat humour with caution. It is difficult to gauge an audience in advance and you may find that a pre-prepared cartoon is inappropriate for that particular audience.

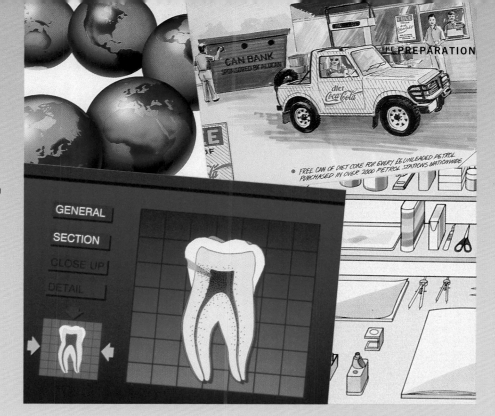

CHARTS AND FIGURES

Graphic representations of facts and figures will often help the audience to grasp a particular point. They can be used in almost any static medium from the flip chart to the slide. Desktop publishing and computer software mean that it is possible to produce increasingly sophisticated and attractive charts both in-house and professionally.

THREE-DIMENSIONAL MODELS

If your product or the object of your presentation cannot be physically present, a model or presentation pack can make all the difference. This may vary from a detailed model of a new dockland development to a cardboard mock-up of double glazing.

It is also possible to copy material such as newspaper clippings or advertisements onto a slide or overhead acetate.

However, make sure that any such material will be clearly legible from the back of the room.

Regardless of the type of visual, always bear in mind that visuals are intended as aids to presentation, not as a diversion. Assess each visual and make sure it achieves the following aims:

- Clarifies and reinforces the message of the presentation.

- Highlights key information.

- Focuses the audience's attention on a particular concept.

- Appears simple and uncluttered.

- Is easy to interpret at a glance.

- Has visual interest.

- Is in keeping with the company's image, or corporate identity.

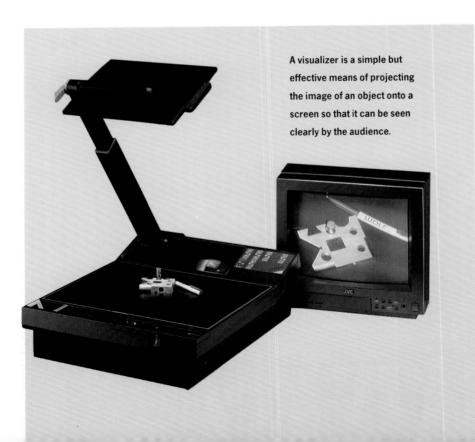

A visualizer is a simple but effective means of projecting the image of an object onto a screen so that it can be seen clearly by the audience.

CHECKLIST

What method will you be using?

- flip chart
- chalkboard
- overhead transparencies
- slides
- video
- multi-media show
- handouts
- models

What type of visuals will be needed?

- Photographs
- Illustration
- Typography
- Charts
- 3-D models
- Other

Professional or in-house?

- budget
- available staff
- suitable equipment
- timing

PROFESSIONAL OR IN-HOUSE

When deciding whether you should call in the professionals there are a number of considerations to bear in mind:

● The audience, the purpose of the presentation, the budget and the venue are fundamental influences on the sophistication and type of visual.

● Do you have the equipment to produce the desired visuals in-house?

● Will the results be professional? Visuals which look amateur will create a bad impression and work against you.

● Will the cost of in-house staff time outweigh the price of a professional?

PRODUCING YOUR OWN VISUALS

There is an increasingly sophisticated array of materials and equipment available for producing your own visuals. The following list is only an indication of the possibilities; new products and ever-more sophisticated computer software make comprehensiveness an impossibility:

● Special film kits will turn any document that can be effectively photocopied into an acetate overlay.

● Charts can be prepared on a computer and printed out – a laser printer will provide a better result than a dot matrix or a daisy wheel.

● Lettering machines will give your type a professional touch.

● Slide masks can be used to create special effects on transparencies – softening edges,

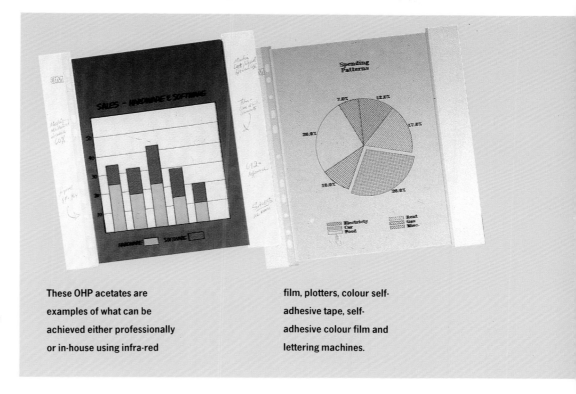

These OHP acetates are examples of what can be achieved either professionally or in-house using infra-red film, plotters, colour self-adhesive tape, self-adhesive colour film and lettering machines.

adding curves and stripes, masking out areas, and so on.

● Colour tapes in self-adhesive rolls can be used to create line graphs on acetate or any other type of film.

● Self-adhesive colour film can be used as a background for an overhead projection or added in small pieces as highlights.

● Computer software will produce colourful visual material in the form of hard copy for handouts, acetate for use with an overhead projector or slides for audio-visual presentations. However, the software available to the public is more restricted in scope than that used by professionals for obvious reasons of cost.

● Desktop publishing systems will enable you to produce printed material of a certain standard of sophistication.

● Simple bindings – comb and thermal – can be produced using fairly simple equipment.

● Lamination machines will coat visual or printed materials in plastic, making them more durable as well as more attractive.

The concept of McDonnell Douglas' world-wide operation is effectively conveyed by a single graphic image, which stands out against the subtle grey background.

Numbers can be used decoratively or to make a specific point. Here colours and imagery combine to produce a tropical effect.

Daring Deeds have given graphic emphasis to their name by using computer effects and trick photography to create an explosive impact which is mirrored in the treatment of the typography.

CALLING IN THE PROFESSIONALS

Whether you are employing professionals to produce slides, a video, a multi-media event or an exhibition stand, it is vital to brief them effectively. There are certain basic rules to follow when briefing a professional:

● By the time you start considering the visuals, you should have determined the aim of the presentation and the expected audience. You should also know what budget you have available. These will be the starting points for any briefing.

● You should have a clear idea of your company's corporate image and make sure that any visuals commissioned reflect the overall image of the company.

● Ideally one person in your company should be the channel of communication between you and the professionals, and that person should have the authority to make decisions, and to authorize expenditure.

● You will know your company and objectives best, while the professional will know what can and cannot be achieved in the particular medium you have chosen. Listen to advice and, if you have confidence in them, let them get on with it.

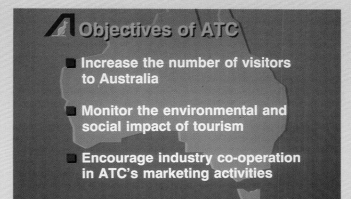

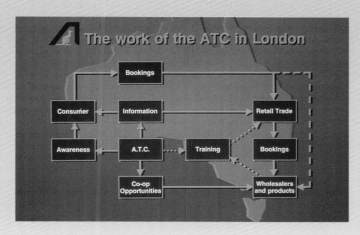

Visual continuity in a presentation can be provided by repeating an image, such as this map, a range of colours, and the company logo (top and right). The bright orange makes a strong contrast with the neutral background.

A computer-generated binder has been effectively combined with a conventional production photograph (below left). Computer animation can be built into a sequence or used on a one-off basis (below right).

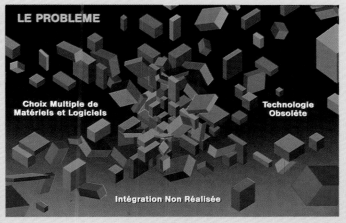

USING THE CORPORATE IMAGE
Companies spend years developing a corporate image, enhancing the favourable aspects of how they are perceived and combatting the less flattering connotations. They spend a great deal of money producing the graphic embodiment of this image. And yet it is amazing how many company presentations neglect to follow this process through by incorporating this valuable image, be it in the form of logo(s), company colours or corporate typeface.

If this area of presentation is neglected, the impression given can be one of sloppiness, or of not caring for your own company. It is imperative that corporate logos are included wherever appropriate, and that the style of the visual matches that of the corporate profile, and of any documentation produced to accompany the presentation.

These slides show a variety of ways of making sometimes complex information accessible and comprehensible while retaining a sense of corporate identity. Two elements in the corporate identity, the logo and the background design, are separated and used to maintain a strong corporate presence on the slides.

The two-colour background design serves as a backdrop to all information. The logo is reproduced in the same position on each slide – giving a sense of continuity and consistency – without imposing itself on the most important element, the information.

Looking at the graphics formats used, the pie chart is invaluable for showing breakdowns of proportionate figures, be they for expenditure or turnover. Colour coding helps to identify the different elements, and the result is a set of complex information made

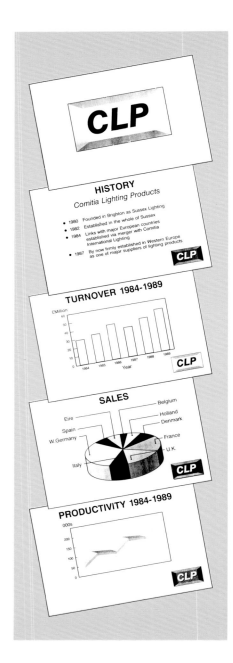

readily understandable and easily comparable, placed in an attractive setting.

Bar charts are ideal for comparing information in chronological sequence, and the use of tints highlights the area of interest: the rise in turnover over previous years.

Text should be used sparingly and should always be placed under a clear heading, so that even the most inattentive delegate will know what is being pointed out. By all means pick out key points as text, but try to see the slides as a set of bullet points to be explained and "sold" by the speaker, rather than as a separate entity.

Tables should of course be clearly calibrated and when showing general trends you can move away from the bar chart format to something a little more interesting to the eye.

If your presentation slides are computer-generated it enables you to produce laser-printed versions. This can be useful during pre-production stages for checking that the concept and approach are right before going to the expense of producing the final product. Laser proofs also make convenient hand-outs for delegates to study later.

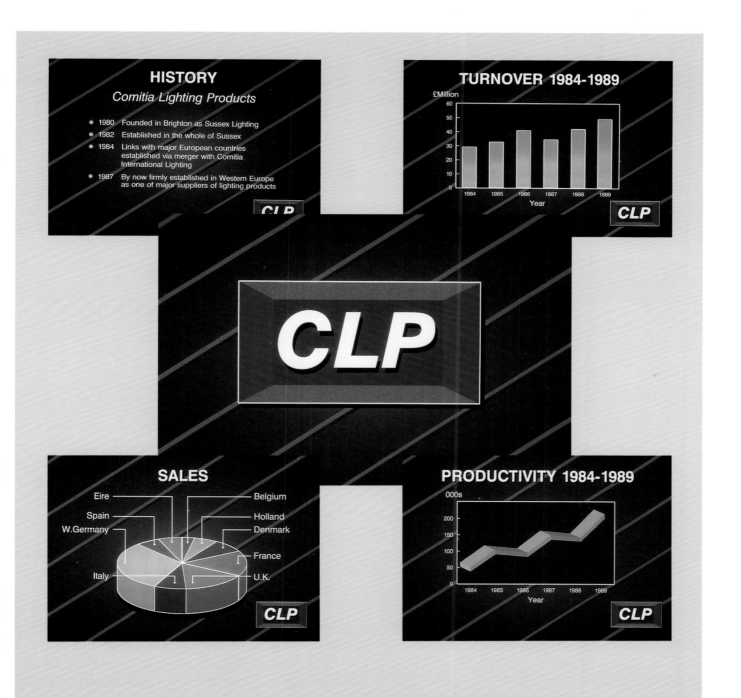

Regardless of the product, the impact of your presentation will increase immeasurably if you can present it visually. Ideally you should show the product itself, but this is not always feasible.

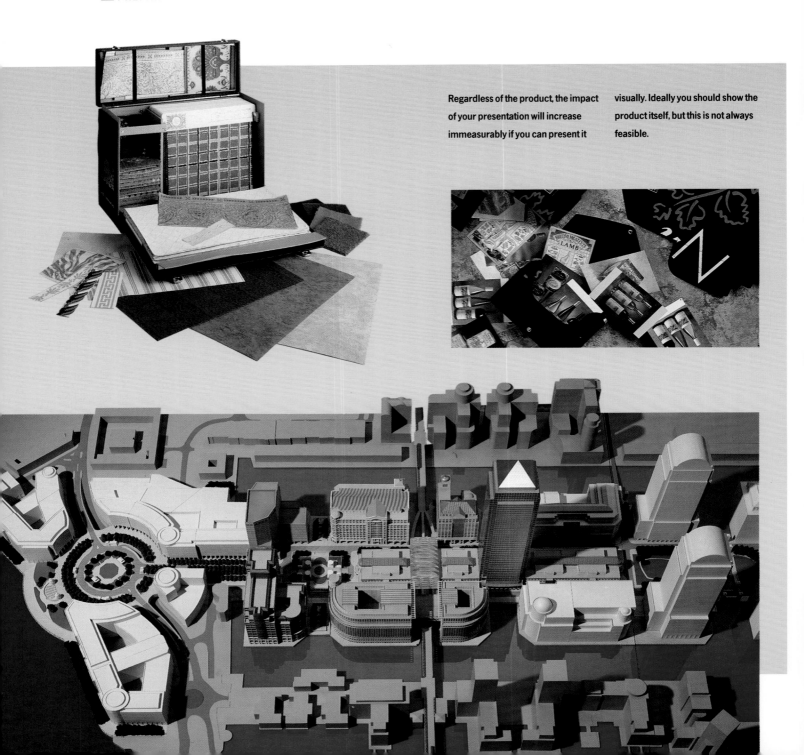

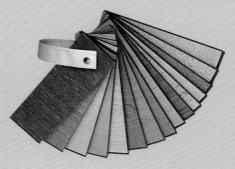

The alternative methods illustrated are just some of the ways you can present a product (clockwise from bottom left): scale model, home decorating swatches, postcard pack, display case, artist's portfolio and promotional books in miniature, pre-printed demonstration flip chart, material samples.

3

FACTS AND FIGURES

Effective presentation of facts and figures will make all the difference to your presentation. The cardinal rules are: make them visual and keep them simple. Several images are often easier to absorb than one complex one.

Some well presented – in other words, easy to assimilate – facts and figures can be a powerful aid to achieving a sale. Mathematical evidence that using your product really does cut costs, is safer, reduces wastage or whatever can be the main weapon in your armoury. Sometimes the necessary information can be easily transmitted and assimilated using nothing more than perhaps the results of some tests.

For example:

"An independent laboratory tested 1,000 of our batteries against two well-known alternative makes. The results were:

Our Brand	– Average life =	10 hours
Brand X	– Average life =	6 hours
Brand Z	– Average life =	5 hours."

The longer life of our brand is obvious and, subject to the price we are asking, offers the best buy."

Unfortunately you will not, in real life, often have such a simple and easy set of figures to work with. It is more likely that, in order to make a comparison, you will need to present a much larger number of figures to the customer. This means that assimilation will be more difficult, and the point you are trying to make may be lost.

Suppose for instance you wanted to compare the profits from investing a sum of £1,000 in three different investment schemes. You are perhaps trying to show that your investment scheme yields the best results. To be convincing about this, you wish to show 10 years results:

	Brand X	Brand Y	Our scheme
1980	100	104	110
1981	90	100	99
1982	91	92	198
1983	90	101	105
1984	87	60	89
1985	103	93	110
1986	66	78	90
1987	92	77	100
1988	85	111	90
1989	101	80	115

If this collection of figures is thrown up on a screen, it will take the viewer a considerable time to run through it and find that in every year but two you beat the opposition.

You could of course show an average for each of the investment schemes which would show that you did better over the whole ten years:

Brand X	–	Average =	90.5
Brand Y	–	Average =	89.6
Our scheme	–	Average =	100.6

These averages are, without doubt, easier to assimilate than the table of figures, but the more numerate customers may still be unconvinced. Your higher average could have resulted from exceptionally good results over the first five years followed by five mediocre years. To avoid this suspicion, you must show the whole picture. Adding the averages to the table still does not relieve the customer of reading through all the figures – indeed the table, including the averages, becomes even more complex.

The solution is to use a chart or diagram. One which would suit this particular case is a bar chart. In *fig. 1*, an example of a bar chart is shown which illustrates the figures, but which is not especially easy to assimilate.

The columns are tall and narrow and, since the differences in the investment results are relatively small, your brand does not show up as having any great advantage.

Greater clarity and impact is given by altering the proportions as in *fig. 2*.

The scale on both axes is larger. This "magnifies" the differences between the columns and makes the whole picture easier to assimilate. Even more clarity could be obtained by leaving a gap between the columns, as shown in *fig. 3*.

This is just one example of using a chart to illustrate what may otherwise be a confusing set of values and to show some of the ways that a chart can be used.

There are a number of other types of illustration which can be used. Their selection depends on the point that you are trying to make and the nature of the comparison or comparisons. The choice of illustration and how you use it will depend on the nature of your message.

OTHER FORMS OF BAR CHART

The vertical style of bar chart has already been illustrated in *figs. 1 – 3*. Another family of bar chart is the horizontal one shown in *fig. 4*. This example shows the values ranked in order. A variation which can be used to emphasize differences is to place the values

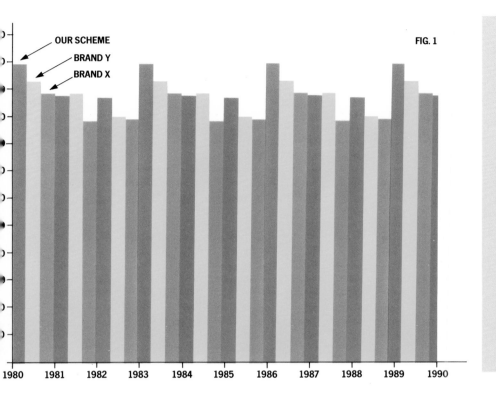

OUR SCHEME
BRAND Y
BRAND X

FIG. 1

1980 1981 1982 1983 1984 1985 1986 1987 1988 1989 1990

These three bar charts are presenting the same information but the choice of scale, layout and colour has a dramatic effect on the audience's ability to assimilate the information. The proportions of the bars (left) make the chart difficult to interpret. Wider bars (bottom left) make it easier for the audience to realize that there are major differences between the brands. Separating the columns (bottom right) makes the situation clear at a glance.

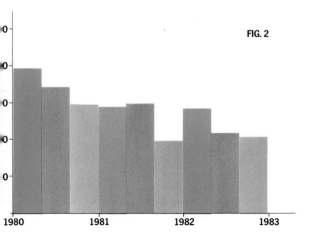

FIG. 2

1980 1981 1982 1983

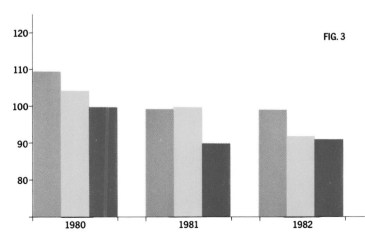

FIG. 3

120
110
100
90
80

1980 1981 1982

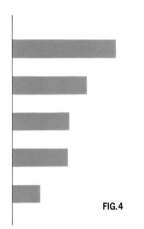

FIG. 4

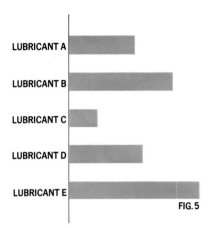

LUBRICANT A

LUBRICANT B

LUBRICANT C

LUBRICANT D

LUBRICANT E

FIG. 5

Horizontal bar charts are an effective means of showing values in order of magnitude (top left) to illustrate, for example, the superior quality of your product compared with competitors. Random positioning (top right) may be an appropriate way to illustrate a particular point. Vertical bars above and below a zero line (bottom left) illustrate positive and negative values. The bar chart (bottom right) is yet another useful variation. In this case, the chart clearly shows the range of characteristics between the products being compared.

in a "random" way as in *fig. 5*.

In this case the relative values of a range of lubricants (say, in terms of engine wear) is uneven, and this is emphasized by the random positioning of the bars.

Both horizontal and vertical bar charts can be used to illustrate negative as well as positive values as shown in *fig. 6*. Such a chart could be used to show that, say, some products have been sold at a loss or that some sales teams have lost customers while some have gained them.

Ranges can also be illustrated as in *fig. 7* where safe operating temperatures for different types of lubricant are shown. Lubricant C is clearly shown to be the most tolerant to temperature variation. Lubricants A, B and D (your competitor's products!) are clearly shown to be inferior in this respect.

The bars can also be used to show an analysis of some sort. In *fig. 8* the comparative cost make-up of using various types of machine are shown.

In this case the comparison has been

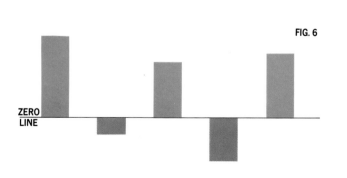

FIG. 6

ZERO
LINE

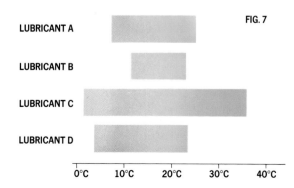

FIG. 7

LUBRICANT A

LUBRICANT B

LUBRICANT C

LUBRICANT D

0°C   10°C   20°C   30°C   40°C

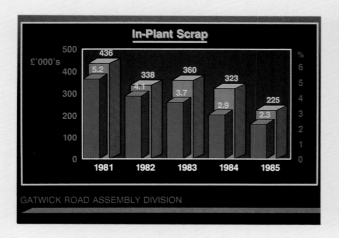

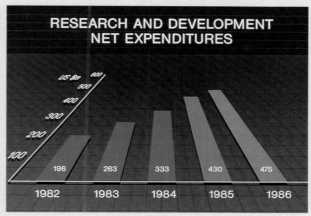

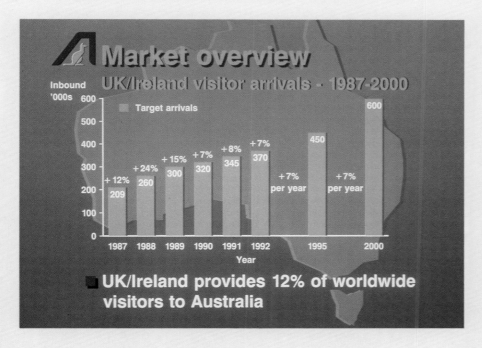

Bar charts and graphs can range from simple sketches on a flip chart to sophisticated computer-generated images. These three examples are typical of the results which can be achieved using desktop equipment and paintbox systems such as Quantel. Software packages provide typesetting, image-making and layout facilities, enabling the designer to devise individual frames and sequences which are output to a high resolution camera and recorded on 35mm transparencies.

Bar charts can be used to illustrate the results of an analysis. The charts (below) show the various costs involved in producing and maintaining several products. The same technique is useful for comparing factors such as the varying times taken to perform a specific task, the mix of raw materials in different grades of a product, or the ingredients used in competing products. Differences may be marked or gradual – this can be shown by using sharply contrasting colours or subtle shading.

made on a percentage basis with each column having the same height. While this draws attention to the variation in how the total cost is made up (labour cost is relatively low for machine A), it does not compare the total costs. This can be done as shown in *fig. 9* by making the height of each column proportional to the total costs for that column.

This type of comparison can be used to show the causes of the cost differences.

Fig. 9 demonstrates that, although the labour cost for machine A is low compared to the other, the maintenance cost is high. It is also immediately clear that both machine A and machine B present high material costs compared to machine C.

Machine C is your product (naturally) and is the cheapest to operate. If you are challenged that your labour cost is higher than for competitive machine A, you could use the chart to illustrate that the designer deliberately allowed for this in order to obtain a substantial saving in materials and maintenance.

Overlapping bars can be used to save space and to emphasize differences even more. An example is given in *fig. 10* where the advantages in terms of wastage and down-time to be had from product C are shown.

Changes over a period of time can also be illustrated, and bar charts can be used to emphasize a point. *Fig. 11* shows a series of values with an additional dotted line to draw attention to the latest value compared to the earliest.

The comparison between 1984 and 1989 would be further emphasized by colouring the whole of the 1984 bar in one colour and using the same colour on each part of the other bars which fall below the dotted line.

Emphasis can also be placed where you want it by using thick arrows to draw the eye, as shown in *fig. 12*. This simple device constantly draws the attention of the audience to the point you are most anxious to make – new improved Whizzo offers the retailer a higher profit margin despite the higher overall price.

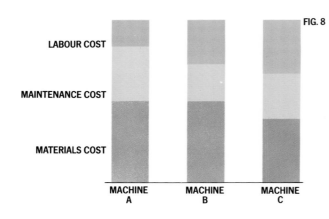

FIG. 8

LABOUR COST

MAINTENANCE COST

MATERIALS COST

MACHINE A MACHINE B MACHINE C

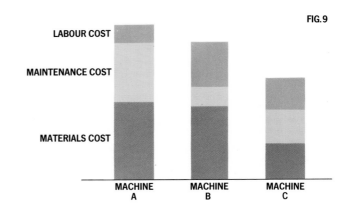

FIG. 9

LABOUR COST

MAINTENANCE COST

MATERIALS COST

MACHINE A MACHINE B MACHINE C

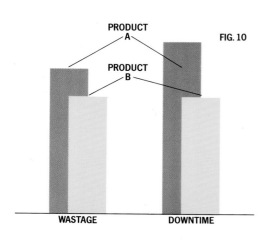

PRODUCT
A

PRODUCT
B

FIG. 10

WASTAGE   DOWNTIME

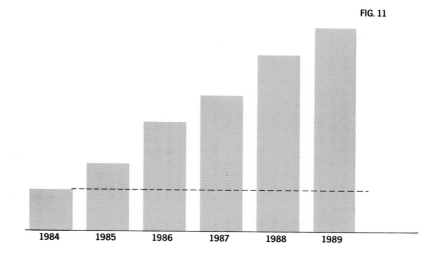

FIG. 11

1984   1985   1986   1987   1988   1989

PIE CHARTS

Pie charts are also useful for making comparisons, especially where the raw figures are hard to assimilate and/or a particular point is to be made.

Suppose for example that an insurance company wishes to emphasize that

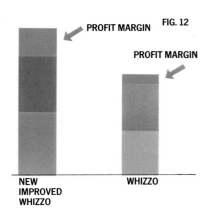

PROFIT MARGIN   FIG. 12

PROFIT MARGIN

NEW
IMPROVED
WHIZZO

WHIZZO

Various graphic devices can be used to emphasize a particular point and fix it in the mind of the audience. Overlapping columns (top left) emphasize the comparison between the products. A dotted line (top right) clearly indicates the difference between the 1984 results and those of later years. Arrows (bottom left) immediately draw attention to a specific point. Colour plays an important role; multi-coloured bars (top right) would be a distraction.

customers' premiums are not being spent either on massive shareholder dividends or on wasteful management costs.

The relevant figures, if they are simply read out, are unlikely to sink in and the comparative order of magnitude is likely to be overlooked. A pie chart makes the point much better – see *fig. 13*.

In this case the smallness of the shareholder dividend is the part you are emphasizing, so it is heavily coloured or shaded to draw attention to it. The immediate visual impression is that it is small compared to the claims paid and to the pie as a whole. If the bonuses paid to clients had been coloured or hatched in the same way as the claims portion, the relative smallness of the dividends would be further enhanced.

At the same time, the return which clients get for their premiums is also emphasized.

Still more emphasis can be placed on a particular slice of the pie by removing it from the circle as shown in *fig. 14*.

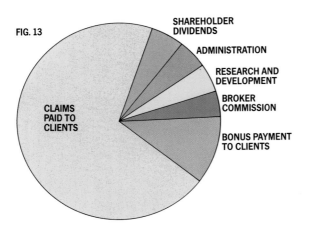

FIG. 13

SHAREHOLDER DIVIDENDS

ADMINISTRATION

RESEARCH AND DEVELOPMENT

BROKER COMMISSION

BONUS PAYMENT TO CLIENTS

CLAIMS PAID TO CLIENTS

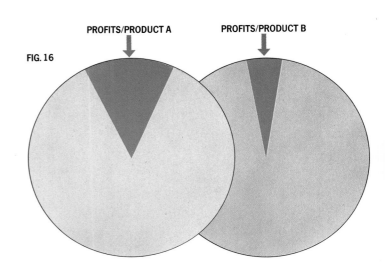

FIG. 16

PROFITS/PRODUCT A

PROFITS/PRODUCT B

Alternatively a segment can be left out altogether. The missing segment immediately draws the eye and can be used for emphasizing a cost saving as in *fig. 15.*

Two pies placed close together or overlapping can also be an effective way of making a comparison.

An example is shown in *fig. 16.* The

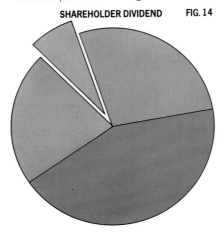

SHAREHOLDER DIVIDEND   FIG. 14

Pie charts are an easy way to assimilate proportions and relative values. Expressions such as "a bigger slice of the cake" and "having a piece of the action" demonstrate the familiarity of the pie-chart concept in everyday life. The basic pie chart (top left) can be altered by partly removing a slice (bottom left) in order to draw attention to it. Completely removing a slice (bottom right) adds further emphasis. Overlapping pie charts (top right) enable you to make comparisons.

overlapping of the charts places the two segments to be compared closer together, thus making it easier to see the difference.

COMBINED PIE AND BAR CHARTS

This is a useful tool when two separate but related ideas need to be illustrated simultaneously. In *fig. 17* the cost segment in

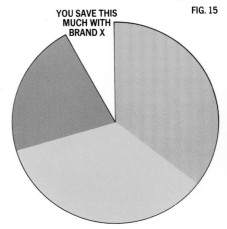

YOU SAVE THIS MUCH WITH BRAND X   FIG. 15

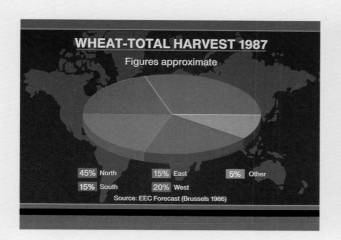

WHEAT-TOTAL HARVEST 1987
Figures approximate

45% North   15% East   5% Other
15% South   20% West
Source: EEC Forecast (Brussels 1986)

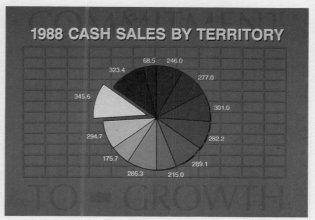

1988 CASH SALES BY TERRITORY

68.5 246.0
323.4   277.0
345.6
             301.0
294.7
             282.2
175.7
             289.1
266.3 215.0

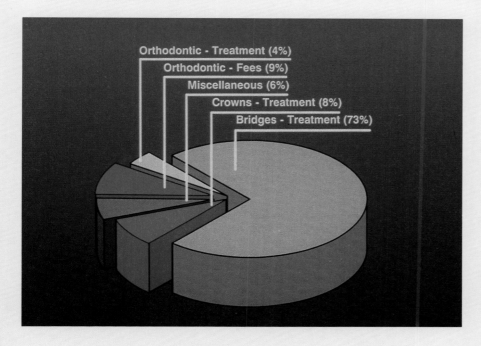

Orthodontic - Treatment (4%)
Orthodontic - Fees (9%)
Miscellaneous (6%)
Crowns - Treatment (8%)
Bridges - Treatment (73%)

Modern technology makes it possible to devise sophisticated three-dimensional pie charts in bright colours against appropriate backgrounds. The professional quality of the design and typography will inevitably impress the audience, but beware of trying to include too much information. Regardless of the level of sophistication in technique, the same basic principle applies – keep the message simple.

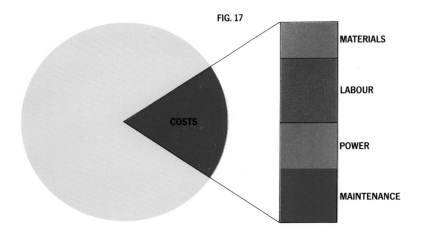

FIG. 17

MATERIALS

LABOUR

COSTS

POWER

MAINTENANCE

the pie is broken down into its various parts in the bar. These constituents of the costs could have been shown by sub-divisions in the pie, but that would have meant four slices of pie instead of one. This would be less easy to assimilate and would have placed the cost elements in the same process of thinking as the other parts of the pie. The bar chart enables you to analyze the costs in detail without confusing the audience.

This separation can be effectively used after showing the pie first without the bar, and then with a second drawing showing the two together. In this way, the presenter can more easily switch the attention of the audience away from the non-costs element to focus on the costs alone. The accompanying narrative might be along the following lines:

"Ladies and Gentlemen, you can see the proportion taken up by the operating costs... (Switches to second slide)...On this slide you can see how those costs are made up. The materials cost as you can see..."

GRAPHS

Yet another version of the picture worth a thousand words, graphs come in a variety of types.

They are commonly used to illustrate changes that occur with the passage of time (see *fig. 18*) and changes relating to differing conditions (see *fig. 19*).

The graph in *fig. 19* has a dotted line to show the operating speed at which rejects are least likely. This type of graph can be effectively used to illustrate, say, the recommended speed for your machine if minimum rejects are the prime target. However, if the scale on the vertical axis shows that rejects are 1% at the optimum speed, but only 2% at maximum speed, the customer may prefer to opt for higher output despite having more rejects.

One of the great benefits of graphs is that variables can be illustrated and permutations of them given easily assimilated values.

There are, though, many cases where there is no apparent, consistent relationship

Combining a pie chart with a bar chart (left) is a useful alternative to dividing a pie chart into a confusing number of tiny slices. Alternatively, one segment of the pie can be examined in greater detail.

Graphs offer a wide range of options to the presenter. They are a familiar concept to most people and, if kept simple, will convey your message effectively. Simple graphs (right above) convey a straightforward message such as the number of sales made over a period of time. Graphs can also clarify relatively confusing situations (right bottom). Drawing a line through the scatter of dots immediately makes it easier to grasp the point being made.

between one thing and another. Graphs can be used to simplify the position and at least establish trends and general pictures.

Suppose for example your reject level was more random in nature – as it is likely to be in

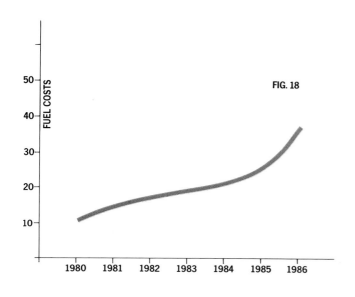

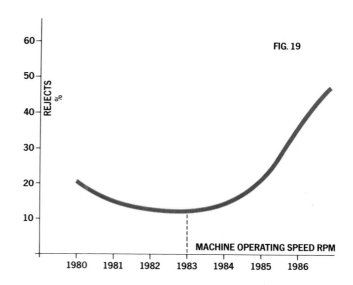

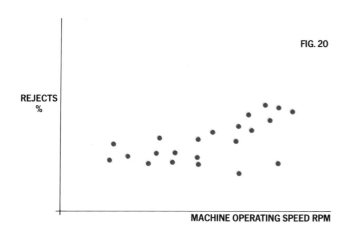

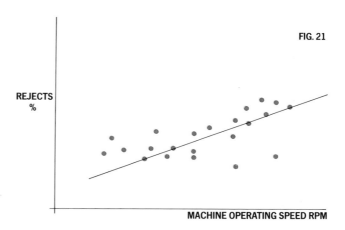

real life. In this case, the relationship between rejects and machine operating speed can be shown by dots as in *fig. 20*.

At first glance (and maybe at second glance), there is no apparent correlation between rejects and speed.

However, if we place a ruler on the dot chart and draw a line through the dots so that roughly half of them are above the line and half below a picture emerges. The line in

fig. 21 shows a general rise in reject rate from left to right, thus indicating a tendency for more rejects to occur at higher speeds. With the use of a flexible curve in place of the ruler, the slight curve downwards (as in *fig. 19*) can

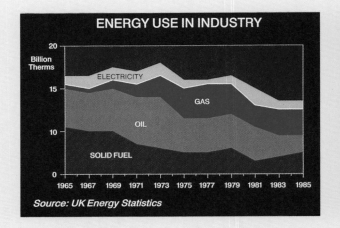

ENERGY USE IN INDUSTRY

Source: UK Energy Statistics

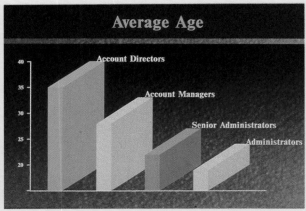

Average Age

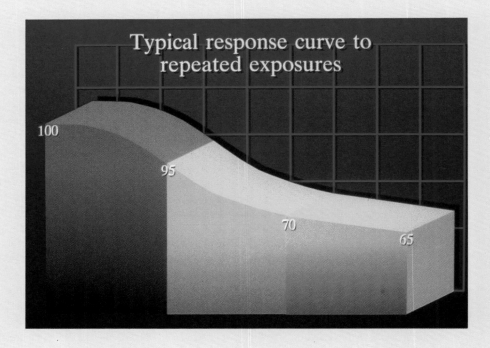

Typical response curve to repeated exposures

As with pie and bar charts, computer-generated graphs can have a strong visual impact. Effective design will make the maximum use of colour, three-dimensional effects and typography to convey your message to the audience. As with all professionally-produced graphics, it is important to brief the designer thoroughly and to approve rough visuals before the slides are produced. In this way, you should avoid the expense involved in making changes to the final product.

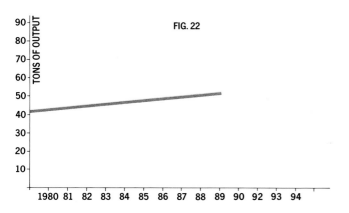

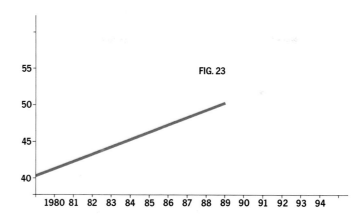

also be illustrated.

As is the case with bar charts, graphs can be drawn using values on the axes which can draw more – or less – attention to the point you wish to make.

The graph shown in *fig. 22* shows a rise in output levels which appears to be unexciting to say the least.

The same information shown in *fig. 23* is presented with much more impact. This results from magnifying the scale on the vertical axis to produce a steeper slope on the graph.

PRETTY PICTURES

Pictures can be used to make effective comparisons. They can be accompanied by figures to reinforce the message. In *fig. 24* the relative sizes of the two oil cans gives the initial impression of the differences in consumption between two machines. The impression is then strengthened and given precision by the labelling of the oil cans – 10 gals. and 2 gals. respectively.

An example of another use of the picture for comparison is given in *fig. 25*, where the

Scales enable the audience to assess the true impact of a steep or shallow curve. A graph without scales is a dishonest way of making a curve seem impressive and should be avoided. Here, combining the same values and different scales creates an immediate impact.

size of the money bags tells the story.

It is important to ensure that the sizes of objects used in a comparative picture are accurately drawn to the correct proportions – especially if no figures are provided to clarify the values being demonstrated.

A more dramatic example of the picture is shown in *fig. 26*. In this case the stopping power of "Sticko" Brakes is being compared

with that of competitive products.

Realism is added by the use of a road scene, a pedestrian crossing and perspective.

Greater impact is provided by the startled look on the face of the pedestrian.

This particular picture could be enhanced with arrows or some other device to show the stopping distance and perhaps a title such as "STOPPING DISTANCES AT A SPEED OF 60 m.p.h."

In *fig. 27* a familiar benchmark – the height of the telephone wires – is used to underline the differences being demonstrated.

This technique enables the audience to "relate" to the sizes of the piles shown, since it is easy to visualize a heap of something which is higher than the telephone wires.

Similar comparisons can be made with other familiar objects such as the height of the Eiffel Tower, the length of a football field, the area of a tennis court and so on.

Pictures, if familiar objects are used, are easier to assimilate than tables of numbers or various forms of chart or graph. They are particularly helpful when dealing with foreign audiences who, although they may speak

THE COMPETITOR'S
MACHINE NEEDS THIS
MUCH OIL

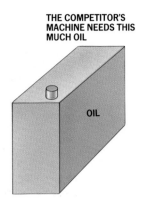

OIL

THE PERFECTO
MACHINE NEEDS
THIS MUCH OIL

OIL

FIG. 24

FIG. 25

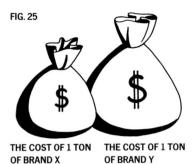

THE COST OF 1 TON
OF BRAND X

THE COST OF 1 TON
OF BRAND Y

Using illustration is another effective means of conveying facts and figures. Bags of money, or piles of banknotes, will not only draw comparisons, but underline the cash aspects of your story. A figure such as 1,472 may mean little to your audience; show them a picture of the Empire State Building labelled "height 1,472" and they have an immediate point of reference. Always bear in mind that images are generally easier than figures to understand and remember.

STOPPING POINT
WITH STICKO BRAKES

STOPPING POINT
WITH COMPETITOR'S BRAKES

FIG. 26

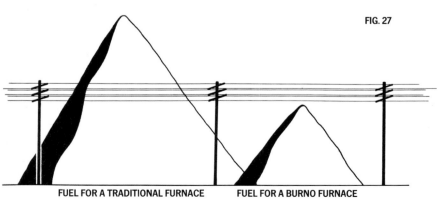

FIG. 27

FUEL FOR A TRADITIONAL FURNACE

FUEL FOR A BURNO FURNACE

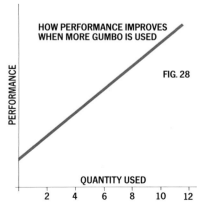

HOW PERFORMANCE IMPROVES
WHEN MORE GUMBO IS USED

FIG. 28

PERFORMANCE

QUANTITY USED

2   4   6   8   10   12

your language fluently, will probably translate any numbers into their own language in order to assess their meaning and value. A well thought out picture can reduce or eliminate the need for this translation, which means that you are less likely to "lose" the audience as you move on to the next part of your presentation.

Pictures also allow you to introduce an element of humour into the presentation without the risk of a spoken joke which may fall completely flat. Humour is a powerful aid to rapport with the audience (providing it is not taken too far) and can make your presentation entertaining as well as informative. The entertainment element, in turn, reduces the chances of the audience becoming bored or tired and can keep them in a relaxed and friendly mood.

TWO WORDS OF WARNING

The head of a new company decided to make a series of presentations to groups of potential clients. He was convinced that a visual message would be most effective, particularly since the benefits of the service he was selling could be expressed in mathematical terms. He prepared a series of overhead projector slides to show the figures analyzed first one way and then another. Percentages, ratios, raw data and summaries were all demonstrated. The slides were drawn by a skilled artist and embellished with colours. Graphs, tables of figures, pie charts and bar charts were all used, and the whole presentation was most carefully rehearsed.

The great day for the first presentation arrived, and an audience of 40 people were treated to a fluent and heavily illustrated message. The presenter finished his piece

and with a happy smile asked his audience for questions. There was a short pause before a lady in the front row said, "That was very impressive, Mr F, but what does it all *mean*?"

This story demonstrates warning number one – Don't *swamp* your audience with charts and diagrams. If there are too many, some will be superfluous and, however well designed they are, the audience will have too much to absorb. Assimilation will be blocked by confusion and mental indigestion, and any unnecessary data will reduce the impact of the valid data.

The illustrations should be kept to the key points that you wish to make, and if possible there should be only one illustration for each key point. If it is not essential, exercise the discipline needed to leave it out.

The second word of warning concerns the *honesty* of your illustration.

Reference has been made to altering the proportions of bar charts and the scales used in graphs in order to emphasize a point. Providing that the chart or graph is *clearly* marked with values so that the audience can *see* what you have done, the technique of adjusting proportions is fair. What is *not* fair is to exclude values which are needed to show the audience the whole truth. In *fig. 28*, there is an example of a wholly dishonest graph. It is dishonest because values on the vertical axis are entirely omitted. The performance could start from a value of say, 10 and rise to say, 1,000. However, there is no way to know if this is the case and performance could be rising from 10 to 11 – or any other figure.

The use of such devices as leaving out the values may fool some of the people some of the time. The chances are that a moderately numerate member of the audience will

challenge the graph and all will be lost.

Even if no dishonesty was intended, it will look as though it was.

THE PROBLEM WITH AVERAGES

Averages are much used in charts and diagrams – often badly.

While an average is a convenient way of expressing the meaning of a large number of values, it can also be entirely unrepresentative of the values. Look, for example, at the following:

Fuel consumption

Vehicle A – 10.4 mpg

Vehicle B – 11.0 mpg

Vehicle C – 11.6 mpg

Vehicle D – 11.2 mpg

Vehicle E – 31.0 mpg

Vehicle F – 29.6 mpg

Average = 17.5 mpg.

To say that the "average vehicle" does 17.5 miles to the gallon would be misleading since none of the sample are anywhere near this figure.

A more reliable statement might be that the modal figure is around 11.0 mpg, i.e., the most *frequently occurring* result is around that level.

Another alternative which may be more helpful is the median figure, i.e., the middle one in a range. The median figure in our table of vehicles and their fuel consumption is 11.6 mpg.

4

THE EQUIPMENT

There is a bewildering amount of presentation equipment — ranging from traditional items such as flip charts to high-tech electronics. It is important to known what is available and to be able to make an informed choice.

There is a vast range of audio-visual and electronic equipment available to presenters, and new products appear regularly. There is, in addition, a wide choice of less sophisticated aids and many "accessories" to give your presentation an appealing touch.

The professional presenter needs to keep in touch with equipment developments – but must not be dazzled by some of the (usually expensive) technology to be found.

Considerable sums of money can be spent on presentation equipment and a cost/benefit analysis is as essential in this field as in any other. An inexpensive item may be as useful and effective in its place as a costly piece of electronic wizardry, and in some cases more so.

The choice of equipment will depend on a number of factors, such as ease of use, portability, reliability and cost. Everyone is limited to some degree by a budget, but this, in presentation terms, need not be depressing. You are not, when selling your widgets, selling your skills in using gadgets or making lights go on and off in an impressive fashion. The aids that you use should be regarded as supports, and not as the be-all and end-all of the presentation. Much can be done on a small budget, and some of the most effective presentations have been based on a very simple and inexpensive kit.

Since your budget is likely to be a prime consideration, the items described in this chapter will begin with the least expensive equipment and work up to the most expensive.

It is equally important that you either know how to operate the equipment or that you hire professionals to do it for you. Your presentation will lose impact and momentum if you are constantly fumbling with your slide projector or presenting blurred images. If you, or a member of your presentation team, is operating the equipment, make sure you are familiar with every aspect, that the equipment is compatible with the presentation room, and that you have taken what precautions you are able to in the case of faults developing.

There are several accessories which, strictly speaking, are not classified as equipment but may contribute to the success of your presentation. In all cases, you will need to decide at an early stage whether you will be using them.

LECTERNS

Some presenters feel more confident when speaking from behind a lectern. A lectern

Lecterns come in all shapes and sizes. The simplest stands on a tripod, while the more sophisticated are boxed in. Microphones are helpful.

may add a certain degree of "authority" to the speaker, but it can also act as a barrier between speaker and audience.

There are lightweight lecterns which offer a good compromise. Their construction hides the speaker only marginally, and they can be helpful as a place for the speaker's notes – avoiding the problem of a fistful of papers. Some lecterns of this type have a microphone attachment, but this means that the speaker cannot move from the spot.

If slides or films are being shown which have no commentary, a lectern with a light attachment can be useful. The room as a whole can be darkened while the presenter has a non-intrusive source of light to read his notes or commentary as he takes the audience through the visuals.

These simpler, lightweight lecterns, including those with a simple sound system, are not expensive. Lectern light attachments can be bought separately.

SHOWBOARDS

Folding showboards measuring about 2 × 2m (6 × 6ft) when fully unfolded are usually made up of three panels. They are useful as a back-up in a presentation to

● Provide additional information.

● Reinforce what was said during the presentation.

● Whet the appetite of the audience before the presentation.

● Entertain the audience during a break for refreshments.

The boards can be used to display photographs, drawings, testimonials, posters,

Showboards can be used to display additional, reinforcing information. Spotlights further highlight specific areas.

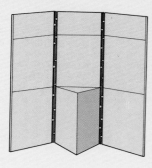

etc. Most convenient are those with a surface which enables the items displayed to be attached with velcro tabs. The tabs make the display easy to change and avoid damage which might be caused by drawing pins or tape.

Some showboards have pedestals which can be placed in front to take brochures and other takeaways, and some are designed to form the background to a reception area.

An additional touch is provided by clamp-on spotlights which can be used to enhance the display.

Showboards can also be used as a

Standing behind a lectern automatically provides the speaker with an authoritative air. Any notes can also be hidden from view making the presentation far tidier.

backdrop to the speaker. In this case the board should not have an enticing display which will attract the audience's attention away from the speaker. A few words in the form of a slogan, the company logo or the brand names of products should be enough.

Care must be taken with the detail on showboards – partly to ensure that there is nothing on them which may conflict with anything the speaker may say. This happened when, during a presentation, some figures for costs were read out to the audience. The figures read out had been revised since the previous presentation, but a showboard, prominently positioned, still showed the old figures. Such mistakes can cause suspicion in the minds of the audience (Are they juggling the figures for our benefit?) or at least indicate carelessness.

Another near-miss occurred when the same company exhibited on their showboard a large map showing the location of the company offices and depots. A few minutes before the presentation was due to start, someone noticed that the coloured adhesive patches representing the offices and depots were in the wrong places. Apparently the person who stuck them on was lacking in geographical knowledge. Fortunately it was possible to correct the board before the customers arrived, but such last minute panics should be avoided by checking the details well in advance.

NAME TAGS

Some people heartily dislike having to wear a name tag. Others prefer them so that they know who they are talking to.

This dilemma can be partly resolved by a classic compromise – presenters wear name

tags themselves, but do not give them to the members of the audience. Much depends on the situation:

● Will every member of your own team know every member of the audience by sight? If not, it may be better to offer tags to avoid the embarrassing business of not knowing someone's name. Failure to be identified is a major blow to anyone's ego and does not encourage a friendly feeling.

If you do use name tags, make sure that the printing on them is large enough to be seen clearly at normal chatting distance. The fact that you have no idea who someone is becomes *very* obvious when you have to bend forward to peer closely at his tag.

● Do the members of the audience already know each other? Obviously name tags are unnecessary if all your audience are from the same part of the same company.

The tags should be easy to fix on the lapel or breast pocket. They should also be suitable for women who are not wearing a suit and have no obvious clip-on place.

At least one manufacturer provides tags which have either clips or pins for fixing them in place. The appearance is otherwise identical.

Adhesive labels are another (and cheaper) alternative, but they should be checked for adhesive quality. A label which sticks to a wool suit may not stick so readily to a fluffy sweater.

THE FLIP CHART

Apart from a chalkboard, the flip chart is perhaps the cheapest and is certainly one of the most flexible aids.

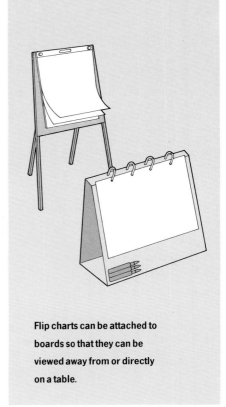

Flip charts can be attached to boards so that they can be viewed away from or directly on a table.

Flip charts are available in two forms: the full size and desk top size.

The full size flip chart is supported by an easel, which can be obtained in lightweight, foldable form complete with a carrying case. This type is used for multiple presentations; they are suitable for audiences up to about 40.

The desk top size is actually intended for one-to-one occasions but can be used with very small groups. This version (also known as a flip-over) will fit into a briefcase and can be placed in front of the customer on a desk or table. The salesperson will then illustrate his message by flipping the pages over one by one.

This of course means that the illustrations

are already prepared – which may or may not be the case with the full size version.

THE PROS AND CONS

The full size flip chart has a number of advantages in addition to its relative cheapness:

● Simplicity of use – no training is required to use a flip chart (except to ensure that the presenter uses large enough lettering for the size of the audience), and no power is needed.

● Flexibility – drawings, diagrams and messages can be prepared in advance *or* as the presentation proceeds.

Some presenters feel that it is necessary to prepare every chart in advance. This is not the case, and some ad hoc writing can be a positive advantage in certain cases. A *skilled* presenter will hold the attention of his audience, or regain it if it has slipped away, by making a bold movement to the flip chart and writing up a few words or sketching a diagram or graph.

The movement will attract the attention of the audience, who will be motivated by curiosity to see what is being written. Sometimes just one word written in large letters can have a major impact. The spontaneity of the act of writing also adds a sense of action and momentum to the presentation.

● "Planned spontaneity"

The presenter who knows his subject well, and can effectively involve his audience, can use a succession of blank flip chart sheets to build up his message.

For example, he can start by writing a

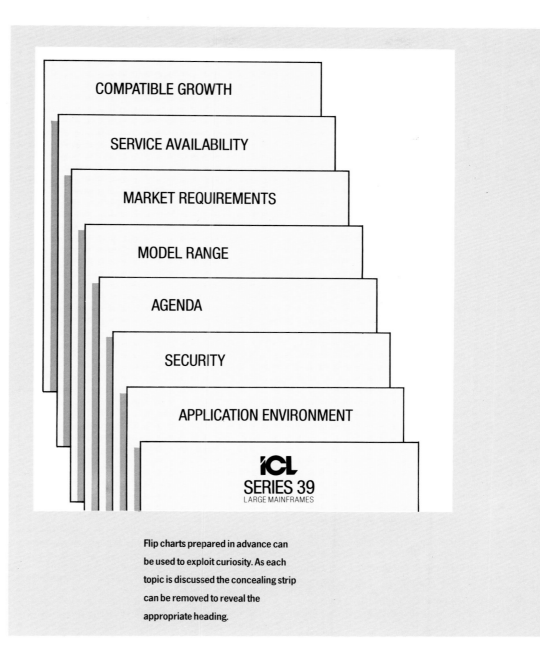

Flip charts prepared in advance can be used to exploit curiosity. As each topic is discussed the concealing strip can be removed to reveal the appropriate heading.

A B C D E F G H I J K L M
a b c d e f g h i j k l m

N O P Q R S T U V
n o p q r s t u v

It is essential when using hand lettering to make sure that the words are legible. Here is an example of a well written alphabet.

feature of the product on a blank sheet and then discuss with the audience the benefits which result from the feature. With suitable questions and subtle prompting, the presenter can tease the audience into listing the benefits.

These benefits can then be written on the sheet against the feature to build up a sales message as if it had come from the members of the audience themselves. The sheet can then be torn from the pad and stuck to a wall or door as a record of what has been concluded.

The presenter now writes another product feature on a new sheet and repeats the process. This way, the audience is continually involved in the presentation and, as a result of having all the sheets constantly on view, is being visually reminded of the benefits which have been revealed.

Such presentations can be exciting for the audience, and properly done, they are very

effective. Sometimes, members of the audience are carried along with such enthusiasm that they suggest benefits which had not occurred to the presenter himself.

The main disadvantages of the flip chart are:

● Size

Its size means that writing on the flip chart must be very large, which means using lots of sheets and creates a flurry of turning pages, or that the medium is limited to relatively small audiences. The size problem is greatest when it is necessary to place a lot of information on a single sheet. A profit and loss account or a long series of laboratory test results are examples. It may be impossible to split the information over two or more sheets without making the data difficult to follow.

● "Scruffiness"

Flip chart sheets tend to roll up in use and it is difficult to stop them from becoming dog-

eared. Flip chart pad carriers which help to prevent this problem are available, but an element of wear and tear usually becomes apparent even then. This means that in general flip charts can only be used once or twice.

● Handwriting problems

Flip charts prepared in advance can be rendered with the aid of stencils to produce professional-looking lettering or diagrams.

If charts are written during the presentation, the user's handwriting and draughtsmanship must be reasonable and certainly legible. This of course is a problem not limited to flip charts. Chalkboards and overhead projectors present the same hazard.

CHALKBOARDS

Many of the comments which apply to flip charts also apply to chalkboards. However, chalkboards are more permanent and do not become dog-eared.

Chalkboards, whether black or white, are normally designed to be permanently fixed in one place, but portable versions are available.

A disadvantage, compared with flip charts, is that space is limited to one board. If it is necessary to display more information, this can only be done by wiping the board clean.

As a result, previous information is lost and so cannot be referred to visually. With a flip chart it is no problem to "turn back".

Some boards are available in a magnetic form which enables the presenter to use magnetic discs, squares and other shapes to build up a graph or chart as he goes along. Alternatively, the whole illustration can be prepared in advance. This normally results in a neater result than a hand-drawn alternative.

PLANNING BOARDS

Planning boards are available in a variety of forms which are normally designed for a specific purpose.

Boards intended for the presentation of statistical information have elasticated graph lines which can be positioned as required against fixed axes. Others use peg-in symbols to illustrate, say, production batches or delivery times against days, weeks or months.

Planning boards are usually made up in advance of the presentation, although the information can be readily altered to illustrate a point being made or, if preferred, the picture can be built up from scratch in front of the audience.

Some planning boards do not travel well as the pegs, labels, etc. can come off rather easily. They are probably best used in a permanent conference room.

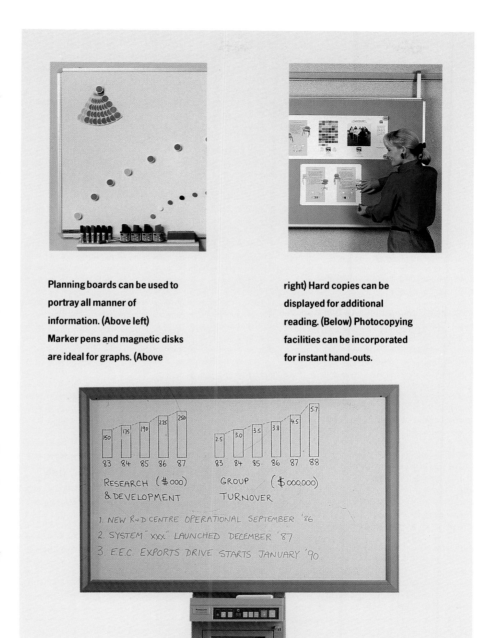

Planning boards can be used to portray all manner of information. (Above left) Marker pens and magnetic disks are ideal for graphs. (Above right) Hard copies can be displayed for additional reading. (Below) Photocopying facilities can be incorporated for instant hand-outs.

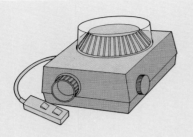

A projector with a carousel is the standard equipment for projecting images onto a screen. At the flick of a button the next slide is put into place. Projectors should always be positioned on a stand so that the image will be projected clearly, above the heads of the audience.

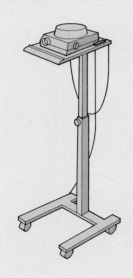

SLIDE PROJECTORS

A good 35mm slide projector can be purchased for a reasonable cost. Ancillary equipment such as a roll-up projection screen, a projector stand and slide holders will more than double your initial outlay, but are still within reasonable guidelines for most companies.

The preparation of slides will of course be an additional cost – one that should not be skimped on, as *quality* slides are essential.

The slides to be used, including those of diagrams, graphs and the like, should be professionally prepared. There is nothing worse than projecting the inadequate draughtsmanship of the sales manager (or whoever) or photographs which have all the hallmarks of amateur holiday snaps.

Professional slides will of course cost money, but in many cases, they will be a one-off cost and can be used over and over again.

Most modern projectors are of the carousel type which allow up to about 120 slides to be included in the presentation. This is preferable to the older slide-in magazine system which takes fewer slides. The carousel also holds the slides more securely, avoiding the ghastly incident when all the slides fall on the floor as the projector is being loaded. Such events do nothing for your presentation.

A remote control device is also a benefit. The presenter, holding the control unit in his hand, can, at the touch of a button, control the focus and move to a new slide. The best machines have a facility for moving back as well as forward, which allows the presenter to remind his audience of something already seen or to flick back when answering a question.

The remote control device also allows the presenter some freedom to move about. This means that he can, if he wishes, stand closer to the audience, join them or move away. With small, informal groups, the presenter can sit down with his audience to create a greater feeling of "closeness" and unity.

The disadvantages of projectors are:

● A screen is required, which can be an inconvenience.

● The images are fixed and cannot be altered. For this reason it is often useful to have a flip chart available as well, so that additional explanation or illustration can be provided in answer to an unexpected question which raises a topic not covered by the slides.

Screens can be permanently attached to a wall and pulled down when needed; or a simple portable device can be erected.

Transparencies always need to
be mounted if they are to be
used as 35mm slides.
Protective casings come in
cardboard or plastic.

SLIDE-TAPE PRESENTATION

At the more sophisticated end of audio-visual
presentations, there are sound tracks and
multi-projector banks to contend with. These
can range from three to 120 projectors, and as
such provide a formidable choice of projected
images. Before looking at these choices,
however, first consider the sound-track.

SOUND

There are several aspects of a sound-track that
need to be taken into account:

● The voice-over. Choosing the right voice or
voices is important – does it sound as though it
is selling, is it just right for explaining
something? If you have the time and the
budget, it is worth auditioning voices. Do allow
sufficient time in the studio for the final
recording, particularly if the voice-over is being
recorded by an amateur; it might take several
goes to get the feel right.

Large, dramatic presentations
require large, dramatic
images. Grouped into banks,
projectors can throw images onto
any combination of screens,
big and small, keeping the
audience on its toes and
driving home the message.

This makes multi-projected images very flexible and keeps the audience awake.

With multi-screen shows, different banks of projectors are focused on different screens. These may be joined together to allow for very large images, or spread around a larger area.

Such presentations require the services of a computer to ensure that each slide is projected at exactly the right moment. The valuable sound track which has been so carefully created will also be keyed into the computer – woe betide you if the system closes down.

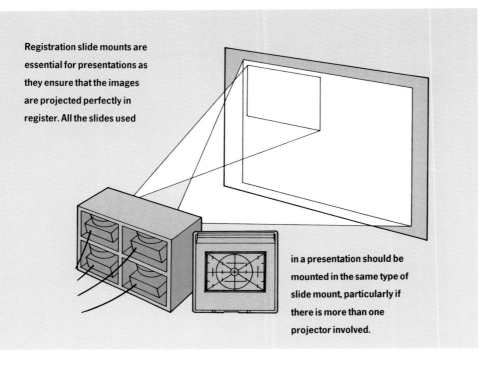

Registration slide mounts are essential for presentations as they ensure that the images are projected perfectly in register. All the slides used in a presentation should be mounted in the same type of slide mount, particularly if there is more than one projector involved.

● The music. Equal care must be taken when choosing the music; not only must it suit the mode of the presentation but it must also be compatible with the tone of the voice-over. Listen to a wide selection of music and once you have established a short list play these to other people involved with the presentation – objective views can be very important. Remember to check that any music you wish to use is out of copyright.

● Sound effects. These should be regarded as the finishing touches and used only sparingly. They can be recorded on location using a good tape recorder or created in a studio using some ingenious methods.

The sequence of events for recording the sound track is:

● Narration.

● Sound-effects.

● Music.

● The entire sound is then mixed and balanced onto a master tape.

USING MULTI-PROJECTORS

Multi-projectors can either be used on single screens or multi-screens. If using the former, not all the projectors will be aimed at all of the screen. Some may be aimed at one part of the screen, while others are aimed at another part.

A splicing block is used to edit a sound tape so that unwanted takes and miscellaneous sounds can be removed. The block rejoins any tape which has been cut.

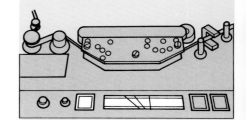

OVERHEAD PROJECTORS

The OHP is possibly the most widely used equipment, but it does have distinct disadvantages.

Costs for the basic machine are higher than for slide projectors. The cost of a screen, the slides (acetates) and various accessories are additional.

Lightweight, portable OHPs weighing about five kilograms (11 pounds) are available at the upper end of the price range.

Another significant variation is the scroll type machine which, by means of a roller attachment, allows the presenter to move to a blank section of film. This latter feature provides a second way in which the OHP can be used. The two methods are:

● Pre-prepared slides

Slides are prepared in advance on acetate film sheets with a usable area of about 280 × 180mm (11 × 7½in). Preparation can be "freehand" using special pens, or a black text can be added by means of a typewriter. Alternatively, an illustration can be prepared on paper and, using a suitable photocopier, can be copied on to the acetate sheet.

These methods rarely result in a high quality image and any defects, such as fuzzy lettering or less than straight lines, are magnified many times when projected on to the screen.

A more sophisticated (and expensive) method of preparation involves the use of a computer and a pen plotter. This method also falls short of the highest quality, although improvements can be gained by using an ink jet printer. The best results – especially in terms of resolution – are obtained by using a thermal transfer printer in conjunction with

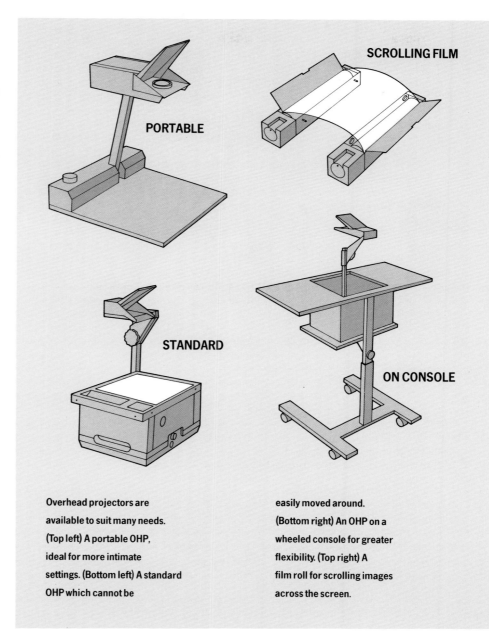

PORTABLE

SCROLLING FILM

STANDARD

ON CONSOLE

Overhead projectors are available to suit many needs. (Top left) A portable OHP, ideal for more intimate settings. (Bottom left) A standard OHP which cannot be easily moved around. (Bottom right) An OHP on a wheeled console for greater flexibility. (Top right) A film roll for scrolling images across the screen.

Overhead projector slides are much larger than those used for slide projectors, but they should also be mounted in cardboard frames. These stop the edges curling up and make them much easier to use.

computer software specially written for the job. An advantage of computer-produced acetates lies in the ability to produce hard-copy versions which can be used as handouts to the audience.

It is helpful to mount the acetate slides in cardboard frames. This makes them easier to handle and prevents marking the slides with fingerprints. It is not unknown for the image projected on the screen to include a magnified thumbprint which is not readily visible on the slide itself.

The frames also provide rigidity to the slide. Unframed slides are prone to curl under the heat of the projection lamp (even if a cooling fan is provided), which results in the edges of the image being out of focus.

● On-the-spot slides

It is possible, using a suitable pen designed for the job, for the presenter to write or draw on a blank acetate sheet while it is on the projector and being shown on the screen. This is much the same as using a flip chart, with the difference that the presenter can write while facing the audience. However, he cannot at the same time see what is appearing on the screen – nor, to some extent can the audience. The image of the presenter's pen and hand are on the screen as he is writing.

This problem needs careful watching when a roll of film (as opposed to single sheets) is being used. Some presenters make the mistake of writing on the film and rolling it on to obtain more space before moving their hand away. This means that the audience has only a partial view of what has been written. In addition, the presenter may block the whole image with his body. This blocking can also happen with flip charts, but with the OHP the presenter may not be so aware of it.

A plotter is the ideal method of reproducing plans and diagrams on film. Different coloured pens and film can be used with ease.

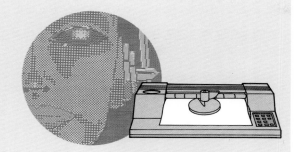

Colour inkjet printers provide transparencies at great speed and high density. As a result, images enlarged many times are still impressive.

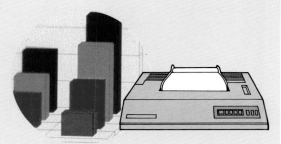

Impact printers or dot matrix printers can easily be employed for creating striking graphics in-house for use as presentation visuals.

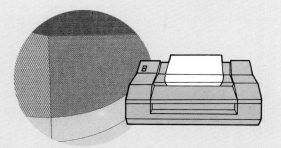

Laser printers are the most efficient and the quietest method of producing visuals. With few moving parts, there is little that can go wrong mechanically.

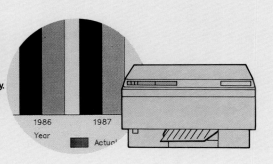

COMPUTERS AND THE OHP

Presentations are more and more frequently organized using a computer. Software which produces charts, diagrams and spreadsheets can provide a variable "real-time" computer screen image for the audience (see p98). The difficulty is that only three or four people can view a computer screen at once. Even then, people sitting or standing at the sides of the group may have difficulty in seeing clearly what is going on. The difficulty, caused by limited screen size, angle distortion and possible light reflection can be solved by linking the computer to an OHP.

This is done by means of a special projection panel and a graphics adaptor port. Many makes of personal computers have a suitable port facility for this purpose.

The result is a projection on a full sized screen which can be seen by a larger audience. Unfortunately, the screen image is likely to lack resolution, as some of the fuzziness of the computer screen will inevitably be magnified. The computer plus OHP system has the additional disadvantage of not being easily portable, but developments in equipment are going on at a fair pace, and more compact equipment will no doubt be available in future.

There is already software available to produce OHP slides and 35mm slides in colour using a personal computer. The same software can be used to create a video via a floppy disk – the videoshow. (Another development is the ability to use a video projector via a floppy disk, but this is moving away from the realms of the OHP.)

It is likely that the developments in computer-linked systems will, in time, replace the traditional OHP presentation. Generally,

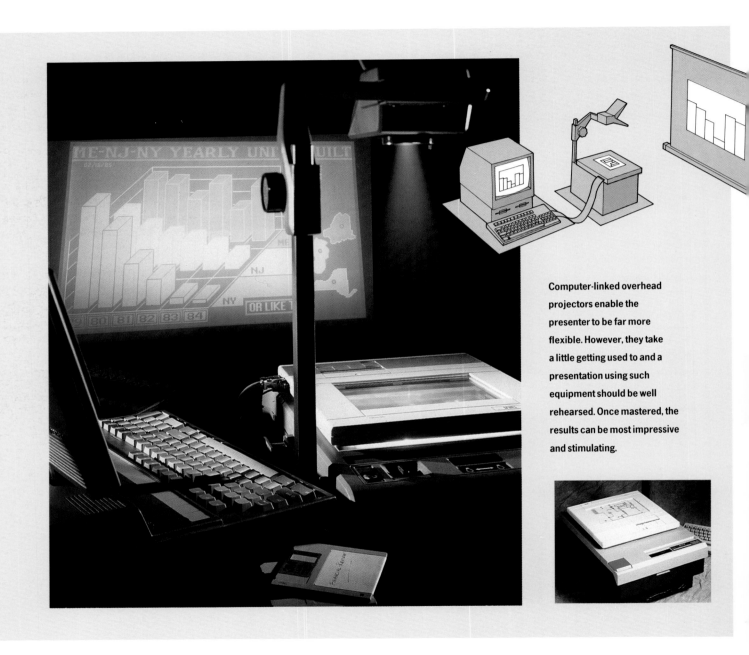

Computer-linked overhead projectors enable the presenter to be far more flexible. However, they take a little getting used to and a presentation using such equipment should be well rehearsed. Once mastered, the results can be most impressive and stimulating.

the OHP is fiddly to use, and the image quality is often poor. It is commonplace to see presenters adjusting the acetate slide on the projector in order to get both top and bottom of the image on the screen. One of the more uncomfortable experiences of presenters – with back to the screen – is to find on turning around that the image is upside down. Worse is to be told by the audience that the image is upside down!

THE VISUALIZER

The visualizer marks a significant step in the development of overhead projectors, for it operates by means of a camera lens rather than just a light reflection. With a visualizer it is therefore possible to place an object directly on the base and the image will be thrown onto the screen as a perfect colour reproduction which will look just like a transparency. Opaque copy such as brochures and articles as well as transparencies and acetates can also be used in this way, making a visualizer far more versatile than an overhead projector.

One presentation featuring an electric shaver included a demonstration where the shaver was dismantled in front of the audience, with each stage simply and clearly illustrated on the screen. The benefits of such a presentation are:

- Less preparation.

- Instant and colourful images.

- The ability to move items around on the screen, making a presentation more flexible and providing some of the interest provoked by a video but with none of the expense.

- Since a visualizer is operated by means of a camera lens, images may be enlarged and reduced at will.

- Automatic focus means that if images are changed on the screen there is no fiddly messing around with moving lenses.

A visualizer combines the flexibility of an overhead projector with the versatility of a camera. Images of objects can be thrown up on screen so that they keep their three-dimensional quality.

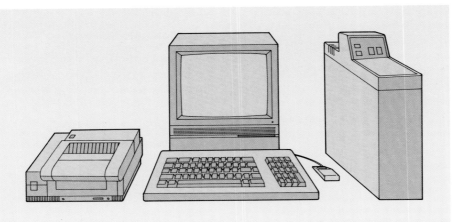

A typical desktop presentation system, comprising a monitor, keyboard, laserprinter and slide writer. With this basic equipment, professional-looking presentations become a reality as images can be brought onto screen and manipulated. Once you are satisfied, the image can be printed as hard copy, or on film.

PRESENTATION GRAPHICS

DTP and video technology have combined to produce the new desktop technology of "presentation graphics" – full-colour text and image design and production for audiovisual presentation through slides or video projectors. Until recently this was only available through specialist companies, using expensive electronic equipment called paintbox (a dedicated computer graphic painting system). However, it is now possible to produce your own graphics in-house if you have a desktop system with the appropriate colour board and monitor and, obviously,

in-house staff who can operate the system effectively. The principal desktop production/delivery systems include the following:

● Frames can be prepared in any available page makeup or paint program and output to paper or film via a laserprinter or imagesetter (a laserprinter that can output line and halftone images as well as typesetting). Colour images can be output via an inkjet or thermal wax printer.

● Dedicated presentation programs can be used to prepare frames of graphics, text and images, to sequence them, and to control the method and time of their delivery. These can be displayed directly on a suitably sized computer monitor, on a screen via a video projector, or output as slide transparencies.

● By interfacing a camera with the computer, images (such as the company logo) which might be time-consuming to recreate using the software package, can simply be photographed and incorporated into the visual.

Slide transparencies can be produced in a variety of ways. Some of them are easily done in-house, others are probably better produced by professionals. However, it is helpful to know what is currently available (remembering that electronic technology is constantly outdating itself!):

● The cheapest method is to photograph the screen directly.

● An electronic RGB (red, green, blue) camera will faithfully reproduce the colour image to a very high resolution.

● An LCD system uses OHP technology to enlarge a duplicate screen image via a liquid crystal diode screen.

● A composite video image can be created by recording the presentation sequence directly onto videotape, for later replay through a large TV monitor or videobeam projector, or as part of a videowall presentation (see p103).

● A composite video or RGB image can be produced directly through a large monitor or videobeam projector.

PRODUCTION OF PRESENTATION GRAPHICS

Whether you produce your own "presentation graphics" or brief a professional, it is important to follow a specific production sequence.

● Analyze the script to decide how best to illustrate it as a set of frames, and what text, graphics and animations will be necessary.

● Write copy for each of the text frames, and captions or annotation for illustrations and diagrams.

● Produce thumbnail sketches which can be worked up into roughs for each visual.

● From these roughs, develop a basic background or grid frame that will help you maintain visual continuity. A basic grid frame might include the following: guides for text, images, bullet points, running title, logo.

● Input your images via a scanner or video digitizer. These will be stored in a suitable format within the software.

● Produce any bar charts and graphs. These can be input from a spreadsheet program or originated as graphics.

● Prepare all text, image and graphic frames. Call up your base grid and paste all your elements onto it.

● Prepare any animated frames with the appropriate graphics package. You can only use animated frames with video computer presentations, although it is possible to animate slide presentations by cross-fading between sequential still frames.

● Sequence all frames and add suitable transition effects, timings, and so on. This stage will depend on whether the presentation is to have a recorded voice-over or be triggered manually to accompany a live commentary.

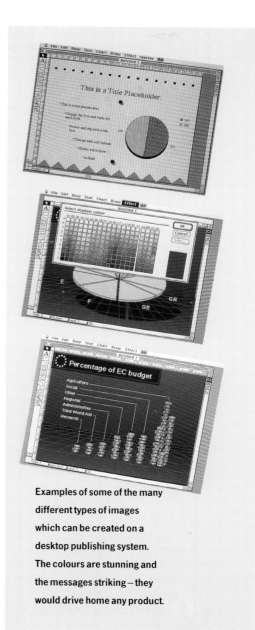

Examples of some of the many different types of images which can be created on a desktop publishing system. The colours are stunning and the messages striking – they would drive home any product.

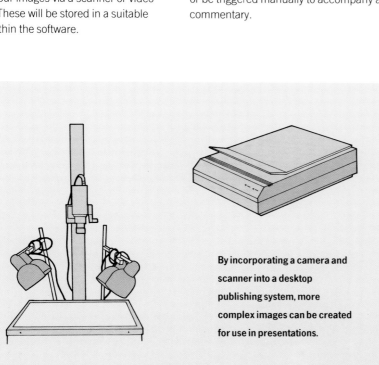

By incorporating a camera and scanner into a desktop publishing system, more complex images can be created for use in presentations.

99

VIDEOS

Professionally prepared video tapes are expensive. In addition, there are other potential disadvantages in using video as well as some (substantial) potential benefits.

● Once a video is made, it is fixed. The message cannot be altered or adapted to suit different types of audience without considerable expense – something which is not too difficult using other presentation methods.

● Videos do not allow for audience participation during the showing. Questions and discussion can follow the showing, but often the presenter needs to repeat a relevant part – if he can find it. Much time can be spent in fast forwarding or rewinding, accompanied by worried comment such as:

"I think it is about here...no...here...not this bit...sorry...you mean this bit...oh, you don't..." etc.

● The time needed to make a video is lengthy and gives the chairman, the chief executive and the rest of the board plenty of time to change their minds about the contents. Many VIP's suddenly discover hitherto unimagined talents as directors or scriptwriters during the course of preparing a video. The results are frequently disastrous and expensive.

● Videos are likely in due course to become outdated. In a fast-moving environment with new products appearing and new markets opening up, it is likely that full value of the video will never be enjoyed.

There are, however, substantial potential benefits.

A *properly* made video is a powerful means of communication which can achieve high levels of assimilation. The use of zoom lenses, library film, microscope camera techniques, time-lapse sequences, slow motion and other effects can produce a series of images not easily achievable by any other means.

In addition, the tapes themselves are light and portable and can, for example, be simultaneously mailed to sales agents and subsidiaries all over the world. A sales promotion can be set up delivering messages which have been checked so that your company controls what is heard and seen wherever it is heard and seen.

There is one video to be extremely wary of – the home-made video.

It is a quirk of human nature that many people see themselves as budding Cecil B. de Milles as soon as making a company film is mentioned. Sadly, very few have the right talents. If they did they would probably be in the film business and not the widget industry.

Here is a fictional, but all too typical, look at the usual results of making your own video:

The story opens with a slightly out of focus shot of the company headquarters building. A blast of stirring music (the entry of the Gladiators?) accompanies this shot and continues while the camera pans (too quickly) down the building. There is a brief glimpse of the company car park before the scene jerks back to the front door of the building. The audience then gazes at 12

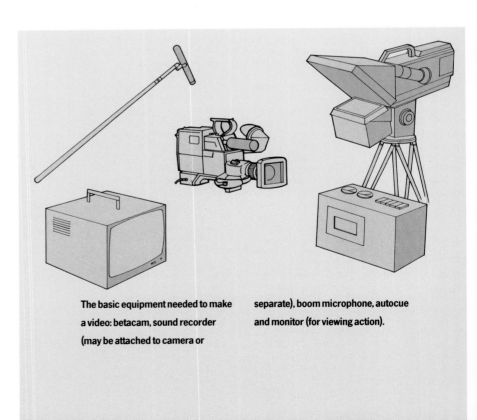

The basic equipment needed to make a video: betacam, sound recorder (may be attached to camera or separate), boom microphone, autocue and monitor (for viewing action).

seconds of blank screen and more music. Suddenly the music stops and they find themselves looking at the smiling head of the chairman. In a style vaguely reminiscent of Charlie Chaplin in jovial mood and with a voice badly modelled on Charlton Heston, the chairman's head addresses the audience.

For 15 minutes (with some jerkiness caused by frequent pauses during filming), the chairman extols the endless virtues of the company, the directors, the staff (loyal unto death), the product, the shareholders and the customers (also loyal unto death – which may make viewers wonder why any new ones are required).

Those of the audience who are still there and still awake when the chairman's head disappears enjoy another 12 second blank period (who forgot the music this time?) before being taken on a lightning tour of the factory. This includes fascinating shots of milling machines, lathes, a forklift truck, two rubbish skips and a fitter scratching his backside in the distance.

The video ends with a shot of a company van disappearing into the sunset and the chairman (now invisible) telling the viewers that this is yet another load of precision-made widgets being delivered to grateful customers.

The whole video is about as entertaining and impressive as Uncle Ted's shots of his holiday hotel in Benidorm.

The golden rule is "If you want a video, employ professionals to make it". Following this rule is expensive, but not as costly as producing an amateur video which is counter-productive.

Multi-media show presented by Abbey National plc.

MULTI-MEDIA SHOWS

Perhaps not too surprisingly, multi-media shows are presentations which combine all manner of visualizing equipment, with or without the use of pre-recorded sound tracks. Banks of projectors with animated sequences, commissioned videos using well-known actors, loud music, flashing lights; they can be extremely lavish affairs, are generally reserved for the largest of presentations and require professional help. Designed to impress, a multi-media show is expensive to put on, and must be slick and smoothly operated in order to achieve its objective. Amateur graphics or delivery will be embarrassing in such circumstances.

However, it is perfectly possible to mount a smaller-scale multi-media show within the confines of a normal presentation suite, such as those found at conference centres. Mixing between several types of visualizing equipment, such as an overhead projector, a slide projector or a video, can result in a very effective presentation. Handsets for such presentations are installed with the equipment and at the press of a button, different media come into play.

Although time-consuming, it can be very enjoyable planning such a presentation. A carefully crafted multi-media presentation should be both varied and stimulating, keeping everyone well entertained and persuaded that your company is highflying and professional.

A typical arrangement of two slide projectors and a video projector which throw the images onto a screen from behind rather than in front.

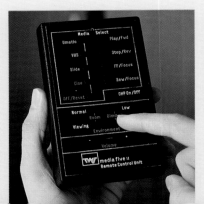

In any one multi-media presentation there might be the need for projected slides, OHP slides and a video. Here, the presenter has everything to hand – all he need do is push a button.

REMOTE DISPLAYS

Once you have commissioned a video it is obviously in your interests to make as much use of the material as possible. In addition to its initial use for a presentation, mailshot or promotion, a video can be a valuable attention-grabber, particularly at exhibitions. In these circumstances, a video can offer the following benefits:

● The moving images will attract the attention and interest of passers-by.

● A video will entertain stand visitors during busy periods when your sales team is occupied.

● A video provides a constant, controllable sales message.

There are a number of commonsense rules regarding the use of video equipment at exhibitions:

● Make sure you have a suitable video, or videos to show. They should carry a simple, accessible sales message, and should not be over-long (a maximum of five minutes).

● Use high quality, reliable equipment. Nothing will tarnish your image faster than an inaudible soundtrack or a fuzzy (or worse, blank) screen.

● Do not let the equipment dominate your stand. However good the video, it cannot clinch a sale. Position it so that it can be spotted from the aisles, but will bring people onto the stand where your sales staff can get to them. If the presentation is too slick, it may become the focus of attention in preference to your sales staff – the very opposite of what you want.

A nine-screen remote video display (above) which neatly encapsulates five images to reinforce a product. (Right) An interactive window with a touch pad. This provides information even when information desks are closed.

● Monitor the sound level regularly. It needs to be audible up to about 10ft from the screen, but no more than that unless you are using it for a major presentation.

Interactive video windows are useful in situations where there is no live salesperson to give information, but are obviously limited in what they can achieve.

Video-walls (a bank of TV monitors) are a spectacular way of using slides and videos, but they can only be effective within a large space. Programmes for video walls have to be professionally produced and edited which makes them expensive.

OPTIONAL EXTRAS

Some companies offer an electronic "news function" attachment which enables you to add or amend text on the screen at any time. This facility can be used to show price changes, recent orders, latest product availability or prize draw winners. Such changes create the impression that "something is happening" on your stand and can produce an air of excitement.

Interactive video is a novelty device which is usually operated by a professional. A software package is used to create a cartoon character on screen which will talk to passers-by. The package is operated by someone who is out of sight (in a closed compartment with a peephole) but can see the audience. This device will certainly attract attention, but there is a danger that the dialogue may cause offence or make people uneasy – not everyone enjoys conducting such a conversation in public. It may be appropriate in the context of a toy exhibition, but completely out-of-place with a more upmarket product.

WHEN TO USE A REMOTE DISPLAY

Deciding when, or if, you should use a video as a remote display device depends on the following factors:

● If the video is to be created particularly for this occasion, have you got a simple message that can be successfully portrayed in a visually exciting way?

● If you are using an existing video, is it appropriate and of the right length?

● In the context of an exhibition, will the video add to or detract from the rest of the stand?

● Is this a cost-effective means of promoting your product?

EXHIBITIONS

Taking a stand at a trade exhibition can be worth much more than placing advertisements in magazines in terms of the interest that will be aroused in your products. After all, everyone attending a trade exhibition will have some interest in your area, and with good planning your display can be made to stand out from the competitors.

To help you make the decision about whether to exhibit, and at which show, ask yourself these key questions:

● Where do my competitors exhibit? Assuming they have the same target market as you, this will be a reasonable guide to assessing a particular exhibition's suitability for your company.

● Is the show likely to attract my target audience? For example, if most of your trade is in exports, you will want to ensure that the exhibition attracts international visitors.

● What do I want to achieve? If you are a fairly new company to a market, you will wish to build awareness of your presence among potential customers. If you are well-established, you may have a specific product range you wish to promote. Get your priorities right from the start.

You should beware of "trying out" an event for one year to see how it goes. People generally remember if you were at the show. If you are not at the next one, they may assume you have gone out of business! It is more sensible to make a commitment for a few years. If you then find that particular exhibition no longer meets your needs, by all means drop out of it – but write to your customers telling them why they will not find you there. In this way, you can stop a damaging rumour before it has a chance to spread.

If you intend booking a stand at a show you know nothing about, it is important to get hold of as much information as you can about this year's and the previous year's exhibitions before committing yourself. Get in touch with the exhibition organizers (the exhibition hall or conference centre will advise you on who to contact) and ask to be sent the following information:

● An information pack which will include the product guide from last year's show (a valuable piece of information as you can immediately see who attended) and details about this year's.

● Pricing information – this will enable you to decide on what size stand you require.

● Visitor promotion, i.e. what events will be laid on, or what is available for entertaining

When planning your stand, try to make it eye-catching in some way. Passers-by should be able to read your company name and main promotional material from the aisle.

any visitors whom you might choose to invite.

● Which exhibitors have booked already and the maximum number the organizers intend to accept.

● A review of the last show's attendance figures and comments of exhibitors. Ask yourself whether the event is growing, and whether it appears to have a good reputation. All this will give you an indication as to the popularity of the show.

● References which you can follow up if you have any doubts.

BOOKING THE STAND

Once you have decided on your show, it is time to book – booking can never be too soon as some organizers run on a first come, first served basis. If you wish to avoid being stuck away in some remote corner, make sure you do not leave booking until it's too late.

About four to six months ahead of the exhibition, you will be sent an exhibitors' manual – the bible of the show. All relevant information is included and there will be many forms to fill in by given dates. It is essential that these forms are duly filled in and sent off as they are required for such information as:

● Description of your exhibits for the main catalogue.

● Advertisement orders for the main catalogue.

● Tickets, passes and promotional material.

● Additions to the standard shell scheme such as extra panels, shelving, display cases, leaflet holders, staging and counters.

- Application for electrical services.

- Application for unloading and lifting.

- Application for compressed air, water and waste.

- Application for furniture hire. There is always a wide choice ranging from office furniture to more informal patio tables with parasols and chairs and lounge seating. Carpet squares, too, are always available in many different colours.

- Temporary telephone service.

- Application for catering service to stands.

- Application for floral hire.

- Hotel booking form.

- Application for evening entertainments, such as a cabaret evening.

- Application for photographs.

- Application for car parking.

By following the manual, you will find that all your basic needs are catered for and the organizers are there to be contacted if there is anything special which you require or have queries about.

You will need to decide your requirements for your stand early on. This may be a simple question of assembling display materials and ensuring staff are booked into hotels throughout the show. However, think your needs through carefully – one issue which often crops up is hospitality. Do you want to be able to offer your visitors coffee, alcohol, or perhaps a light meal? Will you want to take them away from the gaze of other exhibitors to enjoy this fare? Larger companies in

particular often choose to provide a sophisticated array of drinks and food in the privacy of an enclosed area in the middle of their stand. The disadvantages in loss of open stand space are often outweighed by the air of exclusivity this lends to your meetings – and many visitors will be only too glad to escape

Scale model kits such as these Leitner examples are an ideal means of designing a stand. They are exact replicas of the full-size exhibition stands; both are assembled from pre-fabricated panels which can be easily assembled. The stand can then be individualized by the addition of corporate colours, logos, promotional material, plants, etc.

the heat and bustle of the exhibition for a short while.

There is a golden rule to follow when making arrangements for exhibitions: ensure that one person is in overall charge of the project, from booking space and getting the stand designed, to inviting your customers and ensuring there is sufficient car parking for your chairman. Taking an exhibition stand is a logistical nightmare if there are separate sets of people running about doing their part of the job without co-ordination and monitoring at a senior level.

By putting one person in overall charge of the project, you will also have more chance of achieving the impossible with exhibitions: staying within the budget. Few activities can

soak up money at the pace of exhibition attendance. The stand, back-up material, staff costs and the contingency fund for the occasional hiccup all require careful management if you want to stay within your original budget.

ARRIVAL AT THE EXHIBITION

When arriving at the exhibition to set up your stand, always go straight to the organizers' office to book in. Then visit the stand area to check that everything you requested is actually there. Any last minute panics – perhaps extra furniture is needed or running water required after all – can usually be coped with immediately by the organizers or their contractors.

DRESSING THE STAND

When booking your stand, it is essential to obtain detailed dimensions. The organizers will have provided a specification of the shell scheme being used at the show – not only will this include length and depth, but also the height from the floor to underside of the ceiling grid and the height from the floor to the underside of the fascia panel. Important information indeed if you are planning to fit anything large or high into your space.

If you are appointing your own stand contractors do make sure you pass on this information to them or disaster will undoubtedly strike. If you are using your own designer, the organizers usually like to know the details and may require copies of your plans to ensure that the design fits and that no regulations are being broken.

There is a wide variety of modular shell schemes available for putting together exciting and varied displays at exhibitions and there is no need to hire, say, furniture or flowers from the organizers' contractors, you can always bring your own should you wish to achieve something a little different.

The advantage of the modular schemes is that the design can be planned well in advance and the boards brought in complete, ready for positioning.

When deciding on the appearance of your stand, bear in mind the following:

What image do you wish to portray? That of a small, family firm emphasizing the personal treatment; or are you aiming for a slick, technologically-aware image? Whichever you decide on, remember that the point of your stand is to draw potential customers to it, not push them away – a formal array of besuited representatives can be quite formidable. How are you going to attract visitors to your stand? A few suggestions are:

• incorporate something which moves into the design such as a model or video screen. It should, of course, be in a prominent position.

• make use of a bold colour theme.

• large photographs and labelling, which should be clearly positioned.

• ensure that the stand is neither over- nor under-manned.

• ask your salespeople to talk to each other if there is no one else to talk to.

• do not allow your stand to be put above floor level, even by a few inches. The step this creates is a psychological barrier for potential visitors.

• beware of relying on intricate equipment as

a sales tool. If it goes wrong, even for a few minutes, you lose your key attraction.

• brief one member of staff to welcome all visitors and establish their business. This will ensure they are guided to the right salesperson and will discourage timewasters, of whom there are always many at any show.

• consider some promotional gimmick, such as a posting box for business cards which will be drawn every hour with a bottle of champagne given to the winner. This will attract interest to the stand, and by retaining the business cards, you can later monitor who came onto your stand.

Finally, manning an exhibition stand is gruelling work. Staff are on their feet for long periods, under hot lights, and constantly meeting new people. Do not expect them to endure this for too long: rotate your stand personnel so that you always have a fresh, motivated team. A day or two on the stand will be regarded as a treat; a week at a time is invariably a chore.

IN-HOUSE BROCHURES

You may have your sales literature printed and bound externally. You may also have occasions when your literature will be "home-made", especially if a presentation has to be set up at short notice.

A workmanlike job can be produced with a combination of the right equipment on your own premises. The first essential is to ensure that the printed word looks attractive and is readable. A good investment is a laser printer attached to a word processor. Laser printers can produce "typing" in a form which is close to typeset quality with headings or important wording emboldened or enlarged.

This takes no more time to produce than any other typed or word-processed material and looks professional and impressive.

Desktop publishing systems will enable you to produce more sophisticated in-house material, which (depending on your equipment) can include black and white or even colour pictures as well as type.

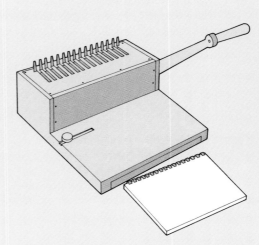

The comb-binding system provides neat slots through which brightly-coloured plastic rolls can be threaded in order to bind together sheets of hard copy. Slots can be varied in size and the secret of success with these machines is not to use too much paper at once.

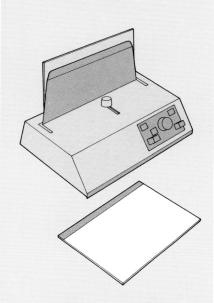

A thermal binding system is a neat and effective way of presenting material, although there is a limit to how many sheets can be used. Colourful covers are available.

BINDING.

A number of pages of home-produced literature will look more impressive (and be easier to handle) if it is bound. Apart from inserting the pages in a ring binder, there are two basic forms of binding. Both sets of equipment cost about the same to buy. The comb binding system is probably the most familiar. The comb binder works by perforating the edges of the papers with a series of small slots and then inserting a plastic "comb" into the slots.

Combs are available for sets of documents up to about 150 pages and binding machines will handle up to the same number of pages.

The top "page" can be a card cover with a title, or it can be a clear plastic sheet through which a typed cover page can be seen.

The thermal binding system which is also suitable for use in the office works using card covers into which the pages are placed by hand. The "spine" of the cover, complete with contents, is then placed in a machine which is electrically heated. The inside of the spine is coated with glue which softens in the heat and the edge of the pages adhere to it. A timer tells the operator when the binding is "cooked" (about a minute) and the finished work can be stacked spine down in a holder to cool. The glue hardens as it cools, resulting in a firm grip on the pages in the folder.

The result is neat and effective and more attractive than comb binding. However, there is a limit of about 12mm (½in) to the spine width, which limits the number of pages which can be inserted.

Covers are available in various colours, with or without apertures for a title page and in sizes from 3mm (⅛in) upward. The thermal binding covers are more than twice as expensive as the binding combs, so running costs differ considerably.

LAMINATING.

You may also have some documents which you do not wish to put in a binder. These can include items which you wish to have a long life, such as instruction sheets, safety notes, product codes or company telephone numbers. All of these are items which you may want your customers to keep in their factories or offices for easy reference and which, if they are helpful and attractive, can continue to sell your image and product. They can be made attractive and resistant to wear, tear and dirt by laminating them with plastic.

Most laminating machines will handle various weights of paper and thin card. They are fairly expensive, but can be a useful investment if sufficient use for them is expected. A good machine will handle small items such as instruction tags and warning tags and sizes up to 46cm (18in) in width.

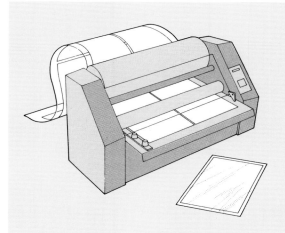

Although comparatively expensive, a laminator can be very useful for those documents which need to last for a long time, are likely to be handled a great deal or be used in a "dirty" environment.

MAKING AN OHP PRESENTATION

An overhead projector is the ideal way of quickly conveying visual information to an audience while maintaining a personal link. But if you are intending to make an OHP presentation, it is essential that you understand the following:

● How to use the available equipment.

● How to make the most of your visual material.

● How to present the information you wish to convey.

USING THE EQUIPMENT

Unlike most other types of projector, an OHP can be used in normal light conditions without ruining the quality of the projected image. Usually, the machine is quite easy to operate. But before making a presentation, experiment with it beforehand to make sure that you know exactly how to turn it on; how to focus it; which way the visuals should be positioned. If you are intending to draw on transparencies during the presentation, practise beforehand – it can be a messy business.

Ensure, too, that the screen is well positioned so that everyone in the room can see it clearly. Finally, check that the image thrown onto the screen is square – it is very easy to project a rhomboid, or worse, if the screen is not exactly parallel to the OHP.

GOOD VISUALS

Other sections of this book look closely at good visuals. Listed here are the essential points to bear in mind when making an OHP presentation:

● Accuracy. Check your spelling and facts.

● Brevity. Visuals should only reinforce, explain or summarize.

● Clarity. Whether you are using words or graphics, always make sure they are large enough.

PRESENTING INFORMATION

To maintain interest at a presentation don't always use the same format for your visuals: endless positioning of text can be very boring. Here are some ideas for varying the procedure:

● Use overlays. A basic outline can be positioned and extra points emphasized by the addition of overlays.

● Masking. The reverse – lift off opaque sheets to reveal an increasingly detailed scenario.

● Animation. Although only simple animation can be achieved on an OHP it is worth experimenting with moving, for example, cut-out letters or numbers to spell words or emphasize statistics. A moving image is a powerful one.

A series of four OHP
transparencies. This one
introduces the product.

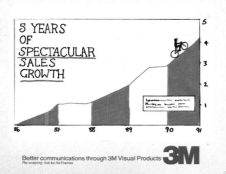

The use of the bike on the
steep incline of sales growth
adds a touch of humour.

Similarly, the mountain
reinforces just how high are
the company's achievements.

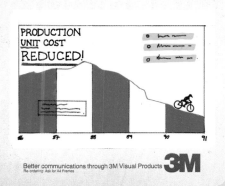

The themes are neatly
continued with the rapid
descent of costs.

MAKING A SLIDE PRESENTATION

Before the actual moment of making a slide presentation, there should be many weeks of planning and preparation. Once the concept has been developed and the decision made as to how the message will be put across, it is time to create the visuals, write the script and select the accompanying music.

Knowing and understanding your audience is vital to all these stages and their possible reaction should continually be borne in mind. Remember that you are there to sell an idea, and this means helping your audience to remember this idea.

Once you have established a budget that suits the occasion you have in mind, you are in a position to decide whether or not you wish to hire professional help. Such help can be invaluable when writing a good, strong script; providing visuals which really work; recording a sound-track that is suitable and clear. However, remember that professionals can be expensive, so the presentation must be one which warrants it.

A production schedule is the next step. Without it, anyone involved in the project will be working to unknown time factors, the results of which could be disastrous. Right at the start of planning, get everyone involved into one room and discuss the outline, deciding who is going to do what and by when.

CREATING THE SLIDES

Elsewhere in this book, there are sections on the many different forms of visual which are available and how to create them. Build-ups and slide sequences can be used to create professional results. Of course, the number of projectors which are available to you will mean that you are either limited to the simplest of fade and dissolve effects, or you can create startling animated sequences. However, regardless of the equipment you should be able to grab your audience's attention and then keep it with the wonderful effects which can be achieved with today's computer graphics.

SOUND

Slide-tape presentations are becoming increasingly popular since, with the addition of sound, a whole new dimension can be added to a presentation.

A sound-track should, if at all possible, be professionally recorded, for scratches and bad links can be incredibly damaging not only to concentration but also to the high-quality image which you will no doubt be wishing to portray.

When making a slide-tape presentation, the sound track is usually prepared first and the visuals fitted to it (the reverse of the video procedure). Remember this when planning the logistics of the event.

Introducing the company. The
logo is strong and the
presentation themes are set.

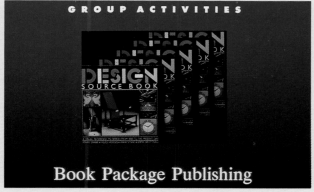

A break down of the company:
book packaging is just one
of the elements.

Other elements include
magazine publishing. The group
activities heading remains.

Finally there are the
marketing and production arms
of the company to introduce.

What the company sets out to
achieve. The header and £10
note emphasize the point.

The movement behind the logo
implies speed – an obvious
benefit when delivering.

Summing up the Quarto Approach
to reinforce the previous
slides and messages.

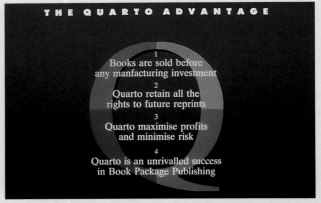

And what of the advantages?
The use of the same background
emphasizes Quarto's image.

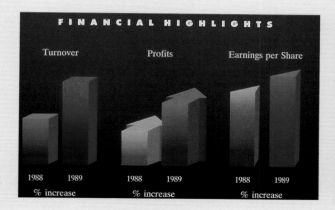

Statistics to back up the
promises. The bar charts
point to the future.

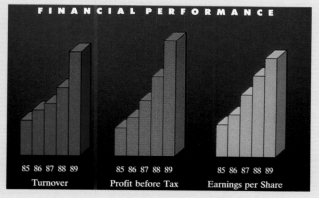

As well as the financial
highlights, the company has
maintained a steady growth.

Strong images help to bring
home the world-wide dealings
of this company.

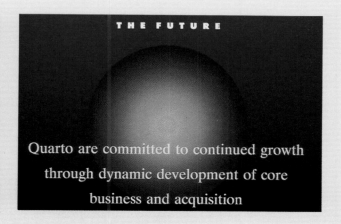

And so to the future. The
words and background image
provide a forceful conclusion.

MAKING A VIDEO

- **The core message you want to put over.**

- **The product and its market.**

- **Timing – when will you use it?**

- **Type of audience.**

- **Other selling methods in use.**

- **Your budget.**

- **Music and sound effects.**

- **Your corporate image.**

The first steps are to consult colleagues in similar areas of business who have had videos produced for them, ask your advertising agency for recommendations, and consult trade journals. However, there are many companies in the business of making videos ranging from poor to excellent. The only sure way to decide on their abilities is to see some presentations they have already made. If the presentations you see are good and impress you, make sure that the person who made them is the person who will make yours. Videos are, like anything else, made by people, not by companies. The best people in the business tend to move around as a result of tempting offers, so make sure that he or she is still there to do your work.

The next best thing – before signing the contract – is to see how the video-makers go about finding out what you want. If one person turns up and asks only one or two questions, you may be heading for trouble. Of course, this could be only a preliminary meeting, but you should be faced with a producer and a scriptwriter at least. You should be asked lots of questions on topics such as those listed in the checklist on the left.

The producer should want to see your brochures, examine and understand your product, see your factory and talk to sales staff. All of this is to give him a thorough feel for your business – something which, at the outset, he probably knows little or nothing about.

Having acquired a good deal of knowledge, the producer can look at it in film-making terms (about which he should know a lot and you probably little) and come up with a proposal.

If this preliminary work is neglected, take care before you sign the contract. Careful pre-enquiry is a hallmark of the real professional.

WORKING WITH THE PROFESSIONALS

Ideally, the producer/director will work in liaison with only one person in your company, who should have a clear brief and a clear line of communication. No other members of your staff (however senior) should be allowed to interfere.

This was how one company started to work with a producer until the first draft of the script was completed. At this stage, several senior people became involved, each insisting on changes to the script. After a lot of argument, a committee was formed and the producer was told to work with them. Weeks went by, with much disagreement and frequent changes of mind about the content of the film. The producer's professional skills were largely ignored by a group of enthusiastic amateurs who lurched from one impractical notion to another.

The crunch came when one member of the committee wrote his own version of the script and proudly presented it. The producer took the script away and returned to face the committee the following day. "Gentlemen," he said, "You can insist on this script if you wish, but it means that the audience will be looking at the same diagram for nine minutes while the voice-over drones on."

Finally, the committee saw sense and allowed the producer to do the job he was trained to do. They got their video and it was a success. It did, however, cost twice as much as originally budgeted as a result of the committee's inference.

THE PROFESSIONAL POINT OF VIEW

It is often helpful to view things from the other side of the fence. An interview with a professional producer of corporate videos on the problems he has encountered when dealing with clients, not only gives valuable pointers towards what you should or should not do when commissioning a video, but also provides an indication of the way your chosen video company should be approaching the making of your video. If your company's methods of research, liaison and budgeting are widely divergent, it might be a warning that the end product will be disappointing.

The two most important points to clarify with a client right at the beginning are:
1. What are they trying to say?
2. To whom are they trying to say it?

It is surprising how often clients decide to commission a video without having a clear idea of the answers. It is important, therefore, for either the client or the video company to undertake research (and to include that in the budget). The video, for instance, may be aimed at shareholders, in-house staff or dealers and may be designed to inform, recruit, train, prepare for cutbacks, answer or instigate questions.

Commodore decided to give their customers a training video to accompany their new computer. These two frames are from the completed video which you can see in production on the following pages.

TITLES: Music and Graphics with title
YOUR COMMODORE COMPANION

EPS 1 - SC

EPISODE 1. SCENE 2 - OFFICE

We mix through to a wide shot of the office.

SUPER: Episode One In Which Tim Opens The Box.

TIM

Great Isn't It?

JOANNE

Yeah really great. We really need another piece of junk in this office.

TIM

Look, my dear this will change our entire lives, It will rid us of all this rubbish for a start.

JOANNE

Oh I see it's an empty box and you're going to fill it with the waste paper I suppose.

TIM

Not quite. But this place is in for a shock. Now if you don't mind I have some work to do.

Tim starts to unpack box.

He is careful and systematic. He lifts out and then spreads on the desk around him the contents listing them as he goes.

Graphic lists the contents in menu form then ticks them off as we see them.

When choosing an idea for a video it is vital to consider the audience and what they will like. A lay audience should not be baffled with jargon or science but, on the other hand, will resent a condescending tone. If it is to be seen by in-house staff or dealers within the company network, you can afford to include trade jargon and abbreviations and to move fairly quickly. In any other situation, it is important to slow down and to explain any specialist terms.

When planning the content of a video, bear in mind that a modern audience expects a video to be informative and, above all, to entertain. A boring video will negate its purpose and be bad public relations. There are two ingredients in particular which can be disastrous to any video.

• Many clients will ask for graphs and figures. These should be avoided at all costs except in special circumstances, such as a scientific audience. Figures, in general, are boring, they are difficult to assimilate in a moving medium because you do not have enough time to look at them properly, and they slow down the pace of the video. If you must have a graph, use computer graphics and keep it simple (one or two points only), otherwise keep figures for brochures. It is also worth remembering that words on graphics will have to be translated if you are showing your video in other countries.

• Talking heads are suited to radio but are boring on television. If you have to include interviews keep them brief. Interviews also provide unnecessary translation problems. With a voiceover you can use exactly the same video with a translation and it will look

as good. With a dubbed interview, it will be obvious that the lips are out of sync and immediately you lose impact.

THE BRIEF

The person briefing the video company should be senior enough to make decisions on contents, expenditure, etc. If a junior person undertakes the briefing there are two dangers. The brief may have passed from the chairman, via several senior employees to the junior. In the process it is likely to become distorted and the video company may produce a script which is condemned by the chairman for being irrelevant or missing the point. Secondly, time and money will be wasted while the junior constantly refers back to those in higher authority.

An even greater danger is the committee. The nature of committees is that all concerned feel they should have a say and nothing gets decided. One person should brief, make decisions and be the channel between the video company and the client.

THE PRODUCT

Videos are unusual in that the client will not know what they have bought until they see the final product. Scripts and storyboards will give some idea of the end product but essentially you will have to trust the video company you have chosen. Once you have chosen a video company, based on your assessment of the work they have done, the main criteria for signing a contract with them are: Do you think you will be able to work with them? Do they appear to understand your business (asking the right questions)? Do you trust them? Do you feel they can produce a good product?

BUDGET

Because of home videos, people tend to think that videos are cheap, simple, and easy to produce. A professional video is never cheap; it can be simple if shot by professionals, but then you should expect to pay for that expertise. Beware of video companies which promise the earth, but do not give you a detailed budget. The video company should give you a detailed breakdown of costs covering every aspect from the cameraman's wages for a day to excess baggage if you are shooting in another country. Some of the costs may be estimates, but you should know exactly what you are getting for your money. If you want to cut the budget, then accept that something will have to be removed to compensate – a day's shooting, some location shots, etc.

Typically, the video crew on a shoot includes the following: producer, director (sometimes one person fulfils both roles), production assistant, lighting cameraman and assistant, second cameraman (needed for drama productions such as the one illustrated) and assistant, set designer, electrician, and a runner, or general dogsbody.

Actor reading script;
cameraman lining up shot;
director checking camera.

Boom operator checking sound
level. This is more effective
than using individual mikes.

Camera assistants marking the
shots. This is necessary
because of the second camera.

Clients stationed behind the
sound and visual control units
watching action on the left.

General view of an off-line
edit suite with a bank of
monitors and mixing equipment.

Editor using a mixing and
effects controller to mix
images from several sources.

Engineer operating video
recording equipment in several
modes, changing the formats.

Sound mixing panel with eight
tracks. Note the detailed
editing script.

PRODUCING THE VIDEO

The video company may ask you to provide an initial script as a starting point. The company should then research further and rewrite the script, giving it a storyline and adding interesting snippets of relevant information to enliven and entertain.

Having commissioned professionals, it is counterproductive not to accept their suggestions. The chairman should expect to give the company some of his time, particularly if he or she is to appear in the video. A day's training on autocue, for example, will mean that the chairman will feel at ease on the shoot, the time he spends will be reduced substantially, and the results will be more professional and therefore more impressive to the viewers.

If the client wishes to attend the shoot out of interest that is usually acceptable to most directors, provided you do not interfere. By this stage you should trust them enough to let them get on with the job, unless you are providing specialist advice on your company's equipment (for example, programming a computer).

The video company should make sure that they understand how the client company see themselves, what corporate image they have and whether they want to change it. It is important to point out to the client that the video they are commissioning should be within the context of all their communications from brochure to letterhead, and is therefore conveying the same corporate image. The aim of the video is to communicate – and it is important for both company and client to make sure that the communication is effective.

These then are the basic groundrules when working with a professional film-maker:

● Be clear about the objective of the video and agree this in writing before doing anything else.

● Give the producer a thorough briefing on the type of audience, market, product, etc.

● Agree the level of the producer's authority – which should, as a minimum, include all technical aspects.

● Brief the producer on any limitations, such as information which must *not* be included in the film or scenes which must not appear.

● Give the producer full access to all the factual information he will need and cooperation in the actual filming and interviews.

● Agree on the length of the video and listen to the producer's advice. There is a temptation to make the video too long – 15-20 minutes is far more likely to succeed than 45-60 minutes.

● Don't change your mind about what you want after shooting has started. This can cost you dearly and may result in the producer giving up!

● Agree the budget in advance and be realistic about it. If you really do want shots of your product being used in far-flung corners of the globe or feel that your video should include views from the top of the Empire State Building, you will have to pay for it. The producer can tell you what it costs to send camera crews on location and whether, in his opinion, expensive activities will really be necessary.

The cost of a video, even without expensive location work, will be measured in thousands.

● Agree the date when shooting will start and the date that you should have the finished article.

● Discuss, in advance, sound effects, voice-overs and any music to be used.

It can be tempting to employ a well known actor to speak the commentary and in some cases it is a good idea. However, it is expensive to employ household names, and a good producer will know of less costly people with good, clear voices.

The right music (if any) is important as it helps to set the mood of the video. The choice is best left to the producer who will be aware of copyright limitations. It may be preferable to commission music especially for your video.

● Don't insist on lots of "mentions". Many a potentially good video has been ruined by insistence on mentioning *all* the factories or *all* the VIPs or whatever. A good commentary will be fairly sparse, and gaps will appear to allow the visual image to "speak" to the audience.

In general, treat your producer as you would a portrait painter commissioned to produce an oil painting of yourself or one of your family.

You would tell the painter what sort of portrait you had in mind and would probably discuss ideas with him at some length. You would then leave him to choose the canvas and the brushes. The painter would mix the colours and apply them. The result will depend on his professional skills – not yours.

THE ENVIRONMENT

The environment is a vital part of any presentation. The right setting will make a favourable impression, minimize distraction, enable the presenter to use equipment effectively and be convenient in terms of travel.

Choosing the right location for a presentation is important, for the environment will not only affect the type of presentation you can give but will make an impression (favourable or otherwise) on the audience. There are a number of factors which will play a part in determining where you can hold a presentation:

● Cost.

● Customer's preferences.

● Availability of facilities, such as conference centres.

● Type of presentation planned (i.e. an intimate presentation to a small group using flip charts, or a multi-media presentation to shareholders).

You may, of course, not be able to choose your environment. If you have been invited to make a presentation, the choice of venue is likely to have been made by others and you will have to adapt as best you can.

When determining your budget, you should try to strike a balance. There is no justification for undue luxury – indeed your customers may question your prices if they are too royally entertained. However, there is a minimum level below which your presentation will be at risk. Sleazy hotels in unfashionable locations combined with old and shaky equipment, shoddy home-made visuals and, worst of all, amateur films and videos can result in failure. There is no such thing as a cheap failure, and budgets must be sensible.

The most important requirement is to have a firm budget which has been calculated on the basis of real need and agreed. This budget should allow sufficient funds to meet the necessary standards without penny pinching or going over the top.

THE CUSTOMERS' TERRITORY

Most of us feel more relaxed and comfortable in a familiar place. This means that if you have a choice, meeting your customers in their own surroundings is likely to be most favourable. Your customers will not have to face the inconvenience of having to travel to see you and the possible worries about getting lost or turning up late.

There may be practical difficulties in making a presentation at the customer's premises, but this choice of location is sometimes unavoidable. If several members of the customer's staff are to be present, it is clearly more convenient for them and will save them time and money if you go to them. However, difficulties can arise as a result of your lack of control of the set-up and facilities.

The author was asked to make a presentation to a group of about a dozen people comprising the council of a trade association. A fully-equipped conference room was promised, including the use of a flip chart and an overhead projector. The presentation was carefully prepared assuming that these items would be available. The council decided, at the last minute, that they preferred to meet in a boardroom which had no facilities for visual aids. The difficulties in making a full presentation without the use of the prepared material were explained, but the council secretary blandly stated that other people were using the conference room and the equipment in it.

The result was a less than satisfactory presentation, and great difficulty was experienced in explaining orally information which had been prepared in a visual form.

Such an occurrence is probably unusual, but if a meeting on the customer's premises is unavoidable or indeed is the best choice, some precautions are worthwhile:

● Try to see the room to be used well ahead of time so that you have advance warning of any peculiarities or limitations. The room may, for instance, be too small to set up *and focus* a projector.

● Even if the customer's projector, screen or whatever is offered for use, take your own along as well. This guarantees that you will have the equipment you need and avoids the problem of coming unstuck because the

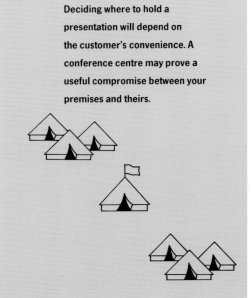

Deciding where to hold a presentation will depend on the customer's convenience. A conference centre may prove a useful compromise between your premises and theirs.

customer's training officer has taken the projector away or it has broken down.

● Take some spare flip chart paper and removable adhesive with you. If all else fails and there is no flip chart easel available, you will still be able to put up your charts.

● Telephone the day before the presentation to confirm the arrangements. Your contact on the customer's team may have given all the necessary instructions, but it is advisable to check that they have been carried out – or have not been changed.

NEUTRAL TERRITORY

The next best alternative is a neutral place such as a hotel or conference centre. You, as the paying customer, can insist on having everything as you want it and can be in a position to offer refreshments. However, double checking all arrangements is still a wise precaution.

Another neutral alternative which is worth considering is a *presentation* centre – as opposed to a *conference* centre.

Presentation centres, which are beginning to appear in major cities, are dedicated solely to presentations, unlike hotels, for whom presentation facilities are a sideline.

The idea is to remove from the customer all the problems of hiring equipment and setting it up, organizing catering, preparing slides, etc. Presentation centres are designed to offer all these services and several others. A wide range of hardware is provided, including such sophisticated items as networked personal computers, front and back projection equipment and video recorders.

The operators of presentation centres claim that they are cheaper than a hotel plus hired equipment. There could also be an advantage in terms of convenience and in the availability of skilled operators for the gadgetry you may wish to use.

OTHER CONSIDERATIONS

Other considerations in choosing your venue will include:

● Ease of travel for the members of the audience.

● Space and physical conditions.

● Heat, light and air.

● Acoustics.

● Decor and atmosphere.

● Possible distractions.

● Cost.

Each of the considerations should receive some careful attention, as they can make a tremendous difference.

EASE OF TRAVEL

The geographical location of your venue will have a link with the timing of your presentation. If, as often happens, people are asked to arrive at 9.00 am for a 9.30 kick-off, then travelling conditions must be favourable. It is not enough to say that the venue is right next to a major road if that highway is choked with traffic from 7.00 am to 10.00 am. No one will thank you for a stomach-churning, frustrating hour in crawling traffic.

A similar problem can arise with the "delightful country mansion" type of venue. Delightful it may be (in spring and summer), but if it can only be reached via a maze of twisting lanes (badly signposted and icy in

If your audience arrives at your chosen venue exhausted and frustrated you will have shot yourself in the foot.

winter), your guests may not arrive in an especially relaxed and happy frame of mind.

Ideally, your combination of timing and location will either make rush hour travel unnecessary and/or the place will be easy to get to. A good train service which your guests can use if they prefer is an added advantage. Some hotels and conference centres provide complimentary transport to and from the local rail station. At all events, provide *detailed* and *accurate* travel instructions with a map which is drawn accurately to scale.

SPACE AND PHYSICAL CONDITIONS

You may be faced with a choice of a room which is either too large or too small. On balance, the smaller room should be preferred – providing it is not cramped to the point of overcrowding and discomfort. Acres

It is important to spend time deciding on the layout which best suits the occasion and the audience. Seating plans will depend on whether the audience is all from the same company, whether you want to encourage participation and the equipment available. These three layouts obviously depend upon the size of the group and the type of equipment being used. All of them enable the audience to watch visuals in comfort and to conduct face-to-face discussions.

of empty space have a disquieting and depressing feel.

There are a number of choices for the layout of the seats. The decision will depend partly on the size and the shape of the room but, assuming this poses no limitations, the basic styles are:

● Boardroom

● Horseshoe shape

● Classroom – in a square

● Classroom – in a rectangle

● Semi-circle.

The boardroom style is suitable for small numbers where the people already know each other or where you want them to get to know each other. The presenter can sit at the head of the table (thus closely relating himself to the group), but if this means getting up and down every few minutes to operate a projector, it can become disturbing.

Make sure that the table is wide enough. Otherwise people facing each other will be too close and almost everyone will have to twist around to see the video screen or other visual aid. This can be uncomfortable and, after ten minutes or so, quite painful.

The horseshoe shape allows for a larger audience than the boardroom style by adding capacity to the "end of the table". People facing each other are not so near to each other and the space in the middle can be used by the presenter to come close to individuals in the audience. This can be helpful when the audience is examining samples "hands-on" or when the presenter wishes to demonstrate something requiring close proximity to the audience.

Conference centres usually provide a variety of venues and facilities, ranging from intimate rooms to impressive halls. Equipment available may range from back projectors, videos and OHPs to multi-media productions. Choosing the appropriate venue will depend on your budget, the type of presentation and your audience.

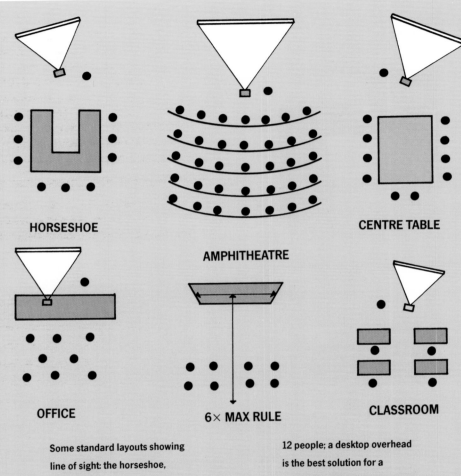

HORSESHOE

AMPHITHEATRE

CENTRE TABLE

OFFICE

6× MAX RULE

CLASSROOM

Some standard layouts showing line of sight: the horseshoe, ideal for 20 or under, encourages discussion; amphitheatre seating on different levels suits a large audience; centre table is ideal in a small room with 6-

12 people; a desktop overhead is the best solution for a small office; the classroom suits a large group or a long session. The audience should be no more than six times the width of the projected image from the screen.

The horseshoe shape is generally a good one for ensuring that everyone in the audience can see the visuals, which can be in the centre of the "open end" and set back a few feet. If a projector is used, it can be positioned behind the "closed end" and directed over the heads of the people sitting at that end. This way, neither the projector nor its stand obstructs anyone's view of the screen.

The square classroom style has a more formal feel, but everyone has an "equal comfort" level, providing that each participant can see the visuals. The head of the person in front can be an obstacle, as can pillars, an overhead projector or even the presenter himself.

The rectangular version of the classroom style can sometimes eliminate these problems, either by placing the long sides of the rectangle across the room or down the room. It all depends again on the shape of the room and limitations (such as power points) to where the visuals and equipment can be placed.

The semi-circle lends itself to a close relationship with the presenter and encourages a friendly, relaxed atmosphere. Line of sight problems are less likely, but the number which can be accommodated is limited unless two or more semi-circular rows can be used.

All the alternatives should be examined in the light of circumstances and the type of presentation that is planned.

HEAT, LIGHT AND AIR

A "reasonable" temperature is important to keeping both presenters and audience wide awake. The optimum, about 20°C (68°F), should be arranged if possible. The author was obliged to give a talk in Cape Town in mid-summer. The room was packed with sweating people, and there was no air-conditioning.

Opening the windows was little help as the air was still and the outside temperature about 38°C (100°F). The only solution was to keep the talk as brief and as lively as possible and to fit in a couple of extra short breaks with cold drinks available. This kind of situation should be avoided if at all possible and preference given to an air-conditioned room. The air which is circulating should be fresh and not from a system which merely recirculates the old air. Even after it is filtered, the old air will come back with a measure of carbon dioxide and other pollutants.

Lighting should be bright enough for people to see to read without straining. Quite often, audiences are placed in semi-darkness to create a "calm and relaxing atmosphere". This may be effective, but it is also soporific and annoying to those who wish to take notes or read the brochure you have given them. There are of course some (rare) occasions when a full scale theatrical performance is required, but this should only be attempted by professionals. Changing the lighting and backing up the visuals with bursts of stirring music is all very well for evangelists or politicians, but rarely suitable for a serious business presentation. Remember that you are offering the benefits of your product, not demonstrating your skills in stage-craft.

TO SMOKE OR NOT TO SMOKE?

Presenters should never smoke while in action. The whole business of finding a cigarette and lighting up is a distraction. It is also difficult to talk fluently when taking a puff on a cigarette every minute or two. Pipe smoking is even worse.

An accountant explaining a system for project costing was a keen pipe smoker. Many of his words were lost as a result of talking with his pipe in his mouth, and every few minutes there was a great re-lighting session. This involved much puffing and grunting, a shower of spent matches and clouds of blue smoke. The audience was not impressed, especially when the answers to questions were held up while the speaker re-lit his pipe. He was perhaps trying to give the impression of careful thought and the benefit of home-spun wisdom, but it did not come across like that.

Whether or not the audience should smoke is a difficult problem. In recent years, the percentage of the population who smoke has fallen to a minority. The problem can be tackled by asking the audience to vote on it or, in large groups, having a smoking area at the back or on one side. The chances are than more people will be annoyed if smoking is allowed than if it is not, and tobacco addicts can be reassured that there will be a break or breaks. Most can hold out for an hour before suffering real withdrawal pains.

ACOUSTICS

With a room which is properly designed and an audience of up to 40 people, it should be possible to manage quite well with the unaided voice. With larger audiences (or if a trial shows that the acoustical properties of the room are bad), a microphone of some sort may be necessary.

The type of microphone which sits on a table is useless when the presenter needs to move about. As soon as he gets up to write on the flip chart, his voice fades away. This can be avoided by using a clip-on microphone attached to the loudspeakers by cable. However, this means not tripping over the cable or allowing it to get entangled with the projector, a chair or something else. The best choice is the radio transmitter type of microphone which requires no cable.

Better still is your unaided voice if you can be heard clearly and distinctly.

DECOR AND ATMOSPHERE

Reaction to the decorative style of the room is subject to wide variation in personal taste. If a choice is being made between one place and

Smoking or non-smoking? The democratic answer is to take a vote. If everyone is from the same company ask the most senior person!

another, it helps to have the opinion of several people so that a range of personal tastes can be applied to the judgement. If the majority say "yes" or "no", that is as good an answer as is needed. There is a tendency to place too much importance on decor, and there is almost always someone in any company who will nit-pick over the colour of the curtains, the wallpaper or the type of chairs provided.

Providing the room is clean and "reasonable", no harm will be done and it is not necessary – or even possible – to satisfy the finer aesthetic sensibilities of every member of the audience.

POSSIBLE DISTRACTIONS

This is a very important subject and, if you find that the conference centre you are thinking about using is right next to the

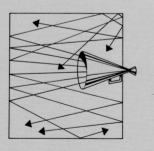

Echoes sound great in the mountains, they will do nothing for your presentation. It is vital to make sure that everyone can hear clearly.

building site of a new factory, beware. Pile driving will begin minutes after you have started your presentation and go on as long as you do. A bulldozer and a collection of pneumatic drills tucked away behind your favoured hotel can also be a warning. Any signs such as this *must* be checked out.

Nearby schools can also be a problem. One sales meeting was disturbed when a couple of hundred children poured into the school playground at break time. The noise brought the meeting to a temporary halt. The whole process was repeated when, in the afternoon, scores of car-driving mothers arrived to collect their offspring. Engines revving, shouted greetings and the noisy emergence of the children once again brought proceedings to a halt.

These are external sources of trouble which are probably beyond your control. They should be avoided by erring on the side of caution and going elsewhere. There are, in addition, internal noise problems which can occur:

● Raucous laughter from an adjacent bar.

● Coffee cups rattling in the adjoining room where refreshments are to be served. This is usually accompanied by audible conversation.

● Crashes and bangs from the kitchens. One hotel in London which has a well-designed and pleasant conference room, unfortunately also has a connecting door to the kitchen, through which comes a continual clatter.

CATERING

You should decide at an early stage whether you wish to feed people at, before or after

your presentation. This will be determined in part by:

● The time the presentation will take place.

● How long you want people to stay – which is linked with how much you have to say.

● The numbers attending.

● The practicality of offering such hospitality.

Assuming you decide to offer a light, midday meal, you have a choice of a formal sit-down meal, or a buffet-style format. Each has its own advantages.

For the sit-down meal:

● You are able to prepare a seating plan to ensure key people are placed next to or near the correct person from your company.

● The overall impression is quite formal and shows you are taking care of your guests.

● You stay in control of the time scale.

● Remember you will need a separate room nearby to offer this hospitality.

For the buffet meal:

● The atmosphere is less formal and people can mix more easily – which can be a drawback if your target audience starts talking with each other instead of with the sales team.

● The costs are generally lower and you have a more flexible menu in case some guests require kosher, vegetarian or other specialist fare.

You will also need to plan tea, coffee or (in a hot climate) cold drink breaks if you are giving a long presentation.

There is no "right" or "wrong" answer to the question of "where". There are pros and cons in each case which need to be weighed up. They should be assessed with the customers' reactions uppermost in your mind.

Check, and then check again. You may have the flip chart but no pens! Do you have the right number of chairs? Where is the power point? Allow an hour before kick-off to ensure that you have everything and that it all works.

CHECKLIST
- Are there enough power points for video players, projectors, etc?
- Will you need extension cables?
- Do the flip chart pens actually write?
- Is there enough flip chart paper?
- Are there enough chairs?
- Is the layout as you want it?
- Have the brochures arrived?
- Is the lighting and air conditioning as you want it?
- Are refreshments as you ordered them?
- Are ashtrays, notepads, pencils, etc., in place?
- Is information giving directions about the location provided?
- Is the reception area set up?
- Have the name badges arrived?

Such attention to detail and preparing for it can make all the difference between an effective performance and a shambles.

YOUR HOME TERRITORY

The final alternative is your own premises, if you have a conference room or other suitable facility. There are a number of things you can do to remove any stress that your customers might experience:

- Make sure that adequate parking space is available and clearly marked, or provide transport from the station if needed.

- Make sure that the receptionist is expecting each guest and provides a warm welcome.

- Offer coffee, tea or some other refreshment.

All these steps will help to make your guests feel at ease *and* important to you.

You will have two potential advantages from being on your own premises:

- The meeting can be set up as you wish.

- Demonstrations or visual aids can be easily arranged, expert colleagues can be used effectively, a tour of the factory can be arranged – or whatever else will assist you in putting over your ideas.

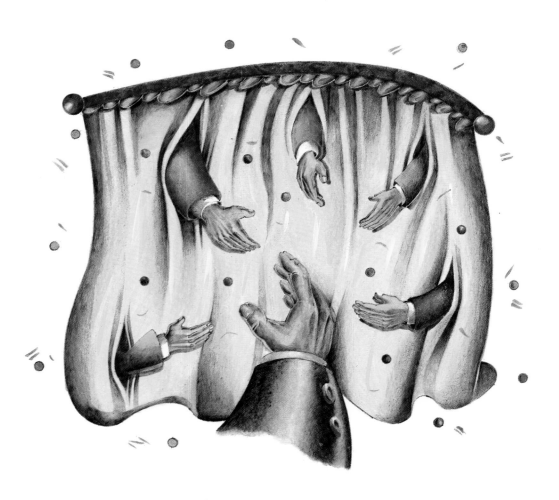

6

CLOSING THE SALE

The final stage is your opportunity to reinforce the most important aspects of the presentation, to answer questions and clear up doubts. If you are selling a product, it is important to follow up promptly by telephone.

However good your presentation may be, there comes a point at which your prospective customer must make a decision — to buy or not to buy. This is the toughest part of any presentation: when the presenter is faced with actually clinching the deal. The discussion stage is over, the points made and the questions answered — now you want a signature on the order form or contract.

Something that makes this happy result more difficult lies within the mind of the salesperson. Everyone who needs to sell to make a living, even the most experienced, have moments of self-doubt. This agony rears its head when you know that you have done a good job, explained all the relevant benefits, but the customer has not given you an order. The solution is to *ask* for the order. If you really have done a full and effective job, then actually asking for the order is likely to be all that is required to get it. Once again it is necessary to think from the customer's viewpoint. He may be quite happy with your product — even strongly attracted to it. However, he is faced with a decision. Help him to make the decision by actually asking for the order. This can be done directly or indirectly.

INDIRECTLY ASKING FOR THE ORDER

A businessman passing a tailor's shop decided, on impulse, to ask about a made-to-measure suit. He went in and was shown a variety of suit materials by an attentive sales assistant. He narrowed his preference down to two types of cloth and asked the price of each. Both were higher than he expected, and he began to hesitate.

The shop assistant, noting the hesitation, realized that his customer was facing a

At the end of a presentation, it may be necessary to repeat some of your most compelling arguments before asking for an order. This drives home your selling message.

decision that he was not too keen to make.

"Which cloth do you prefer, Sir?" he asked.

"This one," replied the customer.

"Very good, Sir," said the shop assistant, picking up an order pad. "Would you prefer two vents in the jacket or one?"

"Oh, two, I think."

"Four buttons on the cuff, Sir?" asked the sales assistant while writing on his pad.

The customer walked out having ordered a suit without actually saying he wanted one because the sales assistant "made the decision for him". By asking which style of jacket the customer preferred, he was acting as if an order had been made. Once the customer had answered the first question he was committed. A degree of firm resolve would have been needed on the customer's part to avoid the question and say, "I don't want a suit".

ANOTHER WAY TO GUIDE THE CUSTOMER

The customer's uncertainty may be due to a lack of information, lack of understanding or even fear of doing the wrong thing. The salesperson who recognizes or suspects one of these can take the customer through a "hierarchy of understanding" to the order placing point. For example:

"You see how the flanged widget reduces friction?"

"Yes."

"...and you are happy with the fuel saving which results from this?"

"Yes."

"I believe you are happy with the price?"

"Yes."

"Fine, I suggest a delivery of fifty widgets is about right for a first order. Shall I put you down for fifty?"

In this "hierarchy of understanding" (which in real life is likely to be rather more lengthy than in the example), the salesperson is reiterating the benefits and ensuring that the customer is fully informed and his doubts are removed.

The customer is unlikely (as in the example) to give a simple "Yes" answer to each question. If he does not, the salesperson has probably hit on an obstacle which needs to be overcome. Having done so, he can move on to another topic, bringing the customer closer to the buying point.

THE "NOT THIS TIME" SITUATION

Sometimes a sale is made by not asking for it *on a particular occasion*. Many buyers dislike being pressured and want time to think about both you and your product. If you feel that your customer is wanting time to think, give it to him.

You must, however, leave the door open for a further meeting when you will close the sale.

"I have given you all the information on the product, Mr Bloggs, and clearly you need time to think things over. I will leave you

If a presentation is continuing in the afternoon after a lunch break always make sure that the table is tidied up in the interim and that clean glasses and refreshments laid out. The audience will be encouraged to view the proceedings with a fresh eye.

in peace and call back next week to get your reaction."

This is a far more productive approach than to persist and risk annoying the customer.

Perseverance and tenacity are important weapons in the salesperson's armoury, but they should not be confused with repetition of the message when it is clearly not the moment when a sale will be made.

THE STRAIGHT REFUSAL

There *will* be times when you will be firmly and clearly told that your product or service are not wanted. This result is always disappointing, but the professional salesperson will not be dismayed by it. The right response to a turn down is a polite "thank you for listening" (no scowls, sulks or sarcastic remarks) and acceptance of the situation. The next step, immediately after the refusal, is to start thinking ahead. The past cannot be recaptured, but the future is waiting – including another assault on the person who has just turned you down. Next time you go to see him, think positively, including all the reasons why he should say "yes" to your proposal. This attitude is much more likely to result in a sale on the second occasion, or the third, or the fourth, or the...

The comments in this chapter so far are generally more applicable to a one-to-one situation. The multiple audience situation is different, and normally requires a more circuitous route to a conclusion. Still, ultimately, the salesperson will need to learn to ask for the order. The particular way to go about it will depend on whether your audience is from one customer company or several.

THE ONE COMPANY AUDIENCE

Ideally you will, shortly after your presentation, be able to get down to brass tacks and ask for the order. During the presentation you will almost certainly have spotted the dominant personality or personalities in the customer's team (if you did not know this already). They will be the people to go for.

If the opportunity to talk about an order does not emerge (for instance, the customer shows no sign of wanting to discuss an order), then such an opportunity must be asked for. If granted, this is, in itself, a buying signal and you can steam ahead. If further discussion is refused, two requirements must be met:

● The opportunity for a meeting in the future.

● An easy way for the customer to place an order when he is ready.

In multiple situations the leader of the customer's team may wish to confer with his colleagues. This is a prudent and natural step to take, and it should not be challenged or scorned. Avoid the mistake made by a brash young salesman unable to hide his disappointment that his audience wanted time to consider the proposals. He turned to the most senior person present and said (petulantly):

"I would not have thought that you were the kind of man who would waste time chatting about things."

Not surprisingly, he lost the sale and was never given the chance to try again. This was a classic example of failing to think from the customer's point of view.

The opportunity for a further meeting can

be requested. If the customer says "no" or prevaricates, he should at least be left with the means to place an order. This could be in the shape of an order form or contract – combined with the name, telephone number and extension number of a contact in your company. The purpose of this is to ensure that if he does decide to place an order, it will not be difficult for him to do so. If he has to write to you asking for a contact or has difficulty in finding the right person by telephone, you are vulnerable to a competitor stepping in and taking the business. A further worthwhile precaution is to have one or even two back-up people to the normal contact in your company.

Secretaries should be primed to pass on any caller to the back-up person if the contact is not available. If the customer has to wait for the contact to come back to him when the contact's trip to Outer Mongolia is over, he may change his mind in the meantime.

THE MIXED AUDIENCE

Presentations to mixed audiences will either take place on your own premises or in some neutral venue. In either case provision, in the form of private meeting rooms, should be made to talk to members of the audience who may wish to meet you privately. It is most unlikely when selling to people representing several businesses that any deals can be concluded publicly.

A further useful provision is to have one or two sales people ready to accompany any interested customers to their offices. This is the place where many people will prefer to be when getting down to brass tacks.

A British sales team working in Northern Germany found that for every presentation made to groups of about twenty people, three or four of them wanted to discuss deals shortly after the meeting – in most cases back in their own offices. Of the remainder about half were responsive to follow up contacts 7-10 days later.

Failure to be ready to deal with a customer immediately after the presentation can be disastrous. Some people will lose interest in your proposals as time goes by, and even a day can make all the difference. However, there will be some people who prefer *not* to make a decision without more thought or consultation with colleagues.

These are the ones to be followed up later.

Once again, everyone should be given a handout package which includes an order form or its equivalent and the necessary contact names and telephone numbers.

A useful tip is to ask each member of the audience for his or her business card. This covers the situation where you had been expecting Mr A, but Mr B turned up in his place. You will need the correct title and correct spelling of the name of each person. The business cards will also provide information on telephone, telex and fax numbers and act as a check on the full and correct company name.

FOLDERS, PENS AND OTHER GIVEAWAYS

Almost everyone enjoys receiving a giveaway even if they pass it on to their children as soon as they get home. The pleasure for some people is out of all proportion to the value – a point recognized by airlines and hotels who dish out a small "gift" with a value only a tiny fraction of the cost of the flight ticket or accommodation. Research has shown that

With small groups, a relaxed questions and answers session around a table (with the presenter seated to add an air of informality) can settle any small worries and doubts that the audience might have. Information can be repeated and further explanations made if necessary.

people receiving such gifts will come back for more, and many choose between airlines on the basis of their giveaways. A small giveaway, of a value so low that it could never be construed as a bribe, may well give pleasure to your listeners and encourage favourable attention.

The other purposes of giveaways include:

● A reminder of your company name, address and telephone number. This can be printed on a pen, pencil, coaster, paperweight, etc.

● A convenient way to carry brochures, specification sheets, order forms and so on. For this purpose there are many types of folder, binder or pouch available at a wide range of prices.

● A means to convey your sales message from members of the audience to their colleagues. This can be in the form of display books with photographs of the product, the latest price list and product description. Remember that the person to whom you are presenting may not be the person who will make the buying decision. These people need the "ammunition" to pass on your information successfully and sell the product or service on your behalf. A well thought out kit in an attractive display book (or binder) will help him to do it.

The cost of the various giveaways should be included in your budget. A reasonable selection might be:

● A ballpoint pen

● A display book

● A pouch for brochures.

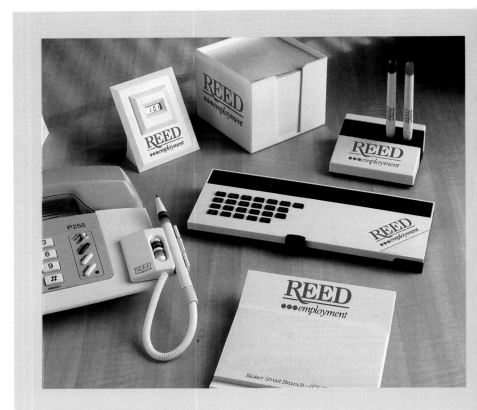

Giveaway items (top left) will act as reminders of a product or your company, as will calendars printed with your company name (top right). Display packs (bottom right) may play a dual role as part of the presentation and as a giveaway. Printed cards (bottom left) make attractive handouts.

Prices will depend heavily on quality, and there are some very costly versions available. However, it is unlikely that spending more than is necessary to provide a tasteful and utilitarian item will increase your sales.

FOLLOWING UP BY TELEPHONE

Your follow-up must be accurate and not spoiled by being addressed to Mrs Tinkle when it was Mrs Tingle who attended your presentation. Generally, a telephone call is likely to be more productive than a letter. Letters can be ignored, lost or added to a pile of pending work. Telephone calls are much more likely to receive attention, and they enable a dialogue to take place.

Having made contact with the right person on the telephone, do not expect him to be eternally grateful that you have called and be desperately anxious to place an order. Your presentation may well have given him all the benefits, and he may have been mightily impressed. However, your call may have reached him smack in the middle of writing a difficult report or examining some worrying budget figures.

The first essential is to enquire if it is convenient to have a conversation at this time – if not, you can suggest an alternative time when you will call again. Care should be taken to assess the mood and reaction of the customer. This is more difficult on the telephone, since you cannot see his facial expression and his tone of voice may be distorted. Nevertheless some gentle probing and assessment is needed.

If he is willing to talk, he can be reminded of the seminar and the subject of an order can be raised. This can be done by asking questions – none of which should start with the question "Why?"

This word often comes across as an implied accusation or criticism:

"Why have we not heard from you?"

"Why have you not placed an order?"

The emphasis should be on the customer's needs and wants:

"What further information would you like to have?"

"How can I help you?"

"Are there any problems which I can sort out?"

If a constructive discussion takes place then, to close the sale, ask for the order.

All the techniques such as fencing and dealing with obstacles may be needed before you get to the closing point so be prepared for it. Alternatively, you may decide that the obstacles are too difficult to deal with by telephone and it will be necessary to suggest a date for a visit. If a visit takes place, you are back to using all the techniques described in Chapter 1. *Good Luck!*

INDEX

D

daisy wheel printer 59
decor 125, 129-30
delivery of presentation 47
demonstrations 9, 26, 44, 45, 127, 131
dependability 19, 21
desktop publishing systems 59, 98, 99, 108
details, obstacles over (hassle) 31-2
difficult personalities 33-4
difficult situations 26-34
discussions 44, 126
distractions 11, 13, 43, 125, 130
dot matrix printers 59, 95
dress 35
duration of transmission 9, 42, 43, 44

E

electrical repair kit 47
emotions 18, 19-22, 28-9, 33-4, 49
    concealed 18, 27-8
    negative 12-15, 23, 28, 29-30, 44
entertainments 104, 106
environment 13, 38-9, 123-31
    checklists 46, 131
    conference rooms 39, 45-7, 125-30
    private meeting rooms 136
equipment 59, 83-121, 124, 127
    choice of 14-15, 84
    spare parts 47
exaggeration 11
exhibitions 104-8
extension leads 47, 131

F

facts 57, 67-81
    warnings about use 81-2
fatigue, audience 12, 44
fears 12-15, 28, 29-30
features, product 22-3, 30, 87-8
feedback 44
figures 57, 67-81, 115
    warnings about use 81-2
films 59
flip charts 57, 58, 71, 86-9
    blocking of vision 94
    checking on 125, 131
    and slide shows 90
floral hire 106
follow-up, by telephone 139
foreign audiences 10, 43-4, 79-81
free gifts 137-9
friendship 19, 20, 32, 35
furniture hire 106

G

giveaways 137-9
graphics *see* visuals
graphs 59, 71, 76-9, 99
    scales 79
    see also charts *and* figures
grid frames 99

H

habit buying, overcoming 28, 29, 30
handouts 46, 58-9, 110, 136, 137-9
    instant 89
handwriting 88
hassle (obstacles over details) 28, 31-2

heating 46, 125, 128-9
honesty 11, 19, 79, 81
horizontal bar charts 68-70
hotels 38-9, 106, 124, 125
humour 10-11, 57, 81

I

illustrations 10, 42, 43, 54-8, 79-82
image, logical 24-6
imagesetter 98
impact printers 95
index cards 51, 52
information 38
    background 8, 39-40
    incorrect 19, 26-7
    lack of 28, 34, 35
    inkjet printers 93, 95
integrity 19-21
interactive video 104
interactive windows 103-4

J

jargon 9
jokes 10-11, 57, 81

K

key words 51, 52
keys to success, three 7-15

Acknowledgments

The publishers would like to thank the following
people and organisations for their assistance and for
providing pictorial material:

Abbey National plc
Aldus UK Ltd
Benoit Jacques
Christv Publishing Ltd/The Original Classic Car Calender
Consultants
Commodore
Crest Hotels Ltd
Easi-bind International
Frances Killingbeck Bain Ltd
G-P Inveresk/Papertalk
Greymatter Design Consultants
Hesselberger Steeden Associates Ltd
Hilton International
ICL United Ltd
Kodak
Leitner
Lemo UK Ltd
Nettle Designs Ltd
Nick Daw, Dox Ltd
Panasonic Business Systems UK
Premium International
The Royal National Pension Fund for Nurses
RVS Ltd
Steve Fletcher
TBS Colour Slides
3M United Kingdom plc
Trenton Group Ltd
TWS plc
Virginia Stoughton of Colour Councillors